THE GREAT LEARNING AND THE MEAN-IN-ACTION

By the same Author

CHINESE PHILOSOPHY IN CLASSICAL TIMES
(*Everyman's Library*)

Published by E. P. DUTTON & CO., INC.

THE GREAT LEARNING
&
THE MEAN-IN-ACTION

Newly translated from the Chinese, with an Introductory
Essay on the History of Chinese Philosophy

BY

E. R. HUGHES, M.A.

*Reader in Chinese Philosophy and Religion in
the University of Oxford*

E. P. DUTTON AND COMPANY, INC.
PUBLISHERS　　　1943　　　NEW YORK

Copyright 1943 by E. R. Hughes
All Rights Reserved. Printed in U. S. A.

FIRST EDITION

¶ *No part of this book may be reproduced in any form without permission in writing from the publisher, except by a reviewer who wishes to quote brief passages in connection with a review written for inclusion in magazine or newspaper or radio broadcast.*

PREFACE

IF any reader, on completing the Introduction and turning over the few other tens of pages, should feel moved to cry out: 'O monstrous! but one halfpennyworth of bread to this intolerable deal of sack,' my response would be that I entirely agree with him. But I think I can make a better case for my sack than perhaps Falstaff could for his. This is the explanation. First, if an old book is really relevant to us to-day, the chances are that it was found relevant by all sorts of people in the ages between ours and the one in which it was written. What those people thought about the book becomes part of its relevance to us; and, indeed, if we miss out their links in the chain of connection, we may easily miss getting linked up at all. Since I could not sleep o' nights through thinking that this generation of mine needed the contact, the only thing to be done was to have a fattish introduction.

Then things began to happen. I planned not more than forty pages, but, when I wrote, forty became a hundred. It was partly the war in Europe and in China, partly certain stubborn facts which refused to be charmed away by the voice of western classical authority. Since I seemed to discount the force of the classical tradition, a tradition which I naturally esteem, I felt obliged to make a placatory bow towards it by going rather more into detail. However, a hundred pages was too much of a good thing. So I rewrote my four chapters—and they turned out longer than ever. I refused to be beaten by this hundred-headed hydra of my argument and had at it again, drained off the more recondite material into a learned article, and wrote the chapters again. This time again over a hundred pages stared me in the face. I then gave up. After all, as the king said to the dairymaid: 'I do like a little bit of butter with my bread.'

To turn to more serious matters: it would have afforded

me the greatest satisfaction if circumstances had made it possible for me to dedicate this book to England's first Chinese professor of Chinese, Professor Tschen Yin-k'o of my own university. The same war conditions which have so far prevented him from coming into residence have deprived me of his critical instruction. The book is that much the poorer. I ask him, therefore, and those others of 'the Learned' to whom I owe so much, to do me the kindness of criticizing the new suggestions which the book contains.

There are two particular debts of gratitude I wish to acknowledge. One is to my colleague, Mr. Wang Wei-ch'eng (Spalding Lecturer in Chinese, 1937–9). This book was first planned as a joint production, and we went together as far as to hammer at the rough drafts of the two translations which I had agreed to make. In the last stages of this hammering, 'September 3rd 1939' sprang upon us, and my colleague decided that he ought to return to China. Thus I had the benefit of his criticisms of my distinctive renderings in the translations, but our collaboration, unfortunately, was prevented from going further. I had no opportunity of discussing with Mr. Wang the materials which are contained in Chapters I to III of the Introduction. As for Chapter IV, we only had time for a few preliminary discussions of the problem of authorship. From these I profited greatly, since Mr. Wang was constant in his insistence that the second half of *The Mean-in-action* had deeper affinities with the first half than was recognized by some modern theories. As I was attracted by these theories, I was driven to a re-examination of the text, with the result that the distinctive opinions I now hold emerged to view. Whether my late colleague would have agreed with these or not, I have no idea. Both in respect to these and to the translations, I have to take the responsibility.

My second debt is to Professor Ku Chieh-kang. Both for his writings and for certain answers he gave to questions of mine six and a half years ago, I owe him much. Now he has increased my obligation to him, for, as I re-examined

The Mean-in-action, I recalled to mind his words at the end of Section 4 in his famous article on the Five Powers (*Te*) (*Tsing Hua Hsueh Pao*, 1930). He flung off there one of those illuminating suggestions of his, in this case that the passage about weights and measures and carts and the forms of the ideographs was part of a eulogy of the First Emperor for his reorganization of the country. This suggestion released my mind: all the pieces of the jigsaw puzzle seemed to slide into place. Not that I believe that the man who wrote that part of *The Mean-in-action* was merely eulogizing the emperor. On the contrary, he was trying to do something very different from mere flattery to him.

In the body of the book I state which texts of *The Mean-in-action* and *The Great Learning* I have taken as the basis of the translations. Since this book of mine is not written primarily for mature western students of Chinese, but is an attempt, in my way, to do for the general reader what Mr. Arthur Waley has done in his inimitable way in his books, there is no need for me to say anything more with regard to the texts. But I should like to urge on less experienced students that they should not allow an element of 'woolliness' in Legge's translations, and occasional signs of impatience in his comments, to blind them to the very real scholarship in his English edition. If that edition were not accessible to students for reference, I could not have left out, as I have done, all those textual and exegetical references which the general reader has every right to insist should not clutter up a book for him.

The end of this preface contains its kernel. It is the confession of a darling prejudice. I do not believe that religion is first and foremost a matter of making certain assumptions about the universe and its origin, drawing certain well-reasoned conclusions, and so arriving at correct knowledge about the Author of this universe. Neither is religion primarily a matter of well-trained emotions and aspirations about certain lofty ideals of conduct and certain hopes of a good time coming for good people. First and foremost, what a man (or a nation) does, not what he thinks and feels, in the face of the major mysteries and uncertainties, of any unexpected and vast exhilaration of joy or shattering distress of mind which cuts in athwart the fabric of his daily life and starts it weaving a different pattern: that is the core of his religion. That being so, a man (or a nation) begins, sooner or later, to think over these crucial acts of his. He wants to know how and why. In other words, he begins to philosophize.

Now the murder is out. I believe that the ordinary man is not only incurably religious—more or less, for, of course, one has to make that distinction—but also cannot help philosophizing: and the trouble about most of us ordinary people is that we are frightened or shy or lazy or badly advised about this inescapable job of thinking. Now in these two Chinese books here translated the reader will find the ideas of some people who were living in a new age: that is to say, an age in which the old order was changing rapidly before their eyes, whilst they were conscious of having new powers of reasoning. The men who wrote these two books used those powers, I should say, with admirable honesty, and so came to conclusions which gave them a new confidence in life and the universe. What they wrote became a system of mirrors in which later generations of wayfaring men and women looked at themselves and their religious acts. Eventually these books came to Europe and had an influence there.

Here, then, I offer these mirrors to you, my readers, believing that as ordinary intelligent persons you do face the major mysteries and uncertainties of your life, that you do act more or less religiously, and, therefore, that you are potential philosophers. That means that you are willing and able, indeed in these days vastly anxious, to apprehend the reality in your universe and the realness in yourselves and your fellow men.

Also, in order that the mirrors might come to you well burnished, I have in Chapter IV of the Introduction taken you into my study, where part of my job is grubbing away at the origins of key words and how they change their meanings. Since you do not know any Chinese, this may seem entirely remote from you. Yet one piece of common sense about philosophy is that we do not really understand what a man was trying to say unless we see pretty clearly what he meant by such and such a word. Now in that new age of which I have been speaking, all sorts of words were getting new meanings tacked on to them. For example, *chun tzu* (which you will find in the translations) first meant a member of the ruling class, and then a man who was versed in the code of honour of that class, and then Confucius made it mean a man of true breeding and honour. So in the new age it came to be used for denoting a true man, an enlightened man, an intelligent, educated man, without much thought as to whether he belonged to the ruling class or not. Since that change obviously means a very important change in a society's ways of thinking, a translator must get the nuances right. It is not fair to anybody just to say 'superior man' every time the word crops up.

And then there is the phrase *t'ien hsia*, literally 'heaven below.' It quite plainly was the word used for the Chou order of fiefs, the kingdom as a whole, but when the big fiefs became virtually independent kingdoms, the phrase still continued to be used. In the mouths of the new thinkers it obviously meant a great cultural unity, in fact, what I have mainly translated it by, namely 'the Great Society.' You miss the significance of many of the statements in *The Mean-in-action* and *The Great Learning*, if you presume the author was thinking of an empire or of the whole wide world. And there is more to it than that. I have in certain key passages translated *t'ien hsia* as 'in this world of men,' or 'in this world of experience.' I claim that as a legitimate rendering of what that thinker had in his mind.

It is clear, therefore, that potential philosophers must keep a wary eye on words. For that reason I venture to urge the general reader to enjoy the first part of Chapter IV.

If, by any chance, he has the idea, which is only too prevalent, that the Chinese do not understand logic, I hope what I have to say there will convince him that this accusation is not true. But then, of course, there is logic and logic, as will appear in the Introduction and the text.

E. R. HUGHES.

OXFORD,
January 1942.

ADDITIONAL NOTE

On 7th July 1940 Professor Chu Ch'ien-chih of the Chung-shan University published, through the Commercial Press, Shanghai, his *Chung-kuo Shih-hsiang tui-yü Ou-chou Wen-hua chih Yin-hsiang* (*The Influence of Chinese Thought on European Culture*). In view of the close agreement between certain of Professor Chu's conclusions and my own, it is necessary to make two matters clear. One is that I had no notion that Professor Chu was working in the same field as I was, nor can I conceive that he had heard of my working in his field. The other is that the manuscript of this book of mine was finished in December 1940. News of Professor Chu's publication reached me early in 1941 through the kindness of my friend, Mr. Hsiao Ch'ien of the London School of Oriental Studies. I included the book in an order sent to Shanghai, but that parcel of books, owing to war conditions, only reached me on 3rd February 1942, seven days before I was due to sail for West China. It was not, therefore, until three weeks later that I was able, on this voyage, to get down to studying these epoch-making researches of Professor Chu.

I can find no serious error in my own treatment, and much to reinforce my decision to select Leibniz and Rousseau, not Voltaire and Dr. Quesnay, as the most significant illustrations of conscious and unconscious Chinese influence on the new European mind. I am not sure, on one hasty perusal, whether Professor Chu, in his treatment, does justice to the Greek and Roman influences at work in that mind or to the influence of the new studies in the natural sciences. On the other hand, his elucidation as a historian of the Jesuit missionaries' predominantly unfavourable opinion of the Sung Li-hsüeh excites my liveliest sense of gratitude. In this matter my own data were seriously inadequate, and I could only surmise that some were for and some against. Also Professor Chu's judicious philosophical appraisement of the extent to which the Jesuits misunderstood and the agnostic philosophers made an unwarrantable use of the Li-hsüeh theories, this, if I may put it so, sets the study of 'Chinese influence' in the right direction. I hope he will feel as I do that there is a substantial harmony between our two sets of conclusions here. In any case, we are agreed, I am sure, that there is an enormous amount of work still to be done, work requiring many kinds of historical and philosophical *expertise*, and that Immanuel Kant is the first person who needs reconsideration from this new angle of approach.

E. R. H.

CONTENTS

	PAGE
PREFACE	V

INTRODUCTION:

    I. *The Mean-in-action* and *The Great Learning* and Ourselves To-day 1

    II. The Changes that come in a 'Great Tradition' and their Predictability and Unpredictability 37

    III. The Society which produced *The Mean-in-action* and *The Great Learning* . . 57

    IV. Who wrote *The Mean-in-action* and *The Great Learning*? 86

TEXT AND NOTES:

The Mean-in-action 105

The Great Learning 145

APPENDICES:

    (i) Leibniz and Chu Hsi 167

    (ii) List of suspiciously late Terms in the suspect Sections of *The Mean-in-action* . . . 171

    (iii) Tzu Ssu in *Mencius* and the *T'an Kung* of the *Li Chi* 172

    (iv) *Wu-wei* (takes no action) in *The Mean-in-action*, Section XI 174

    (v) *Chung Kuo*, the Middle Kingdom: *The Mean-in-action*, Section XVII, and *The Great Learning*, Section VII, 4 175

    (vi) Rousseau and Nature in Family Relations . 176

THE GREAT LEARNING AND THE MEAN-IN-ACTION

INTRODUCTION

CHAPTER I

'THE MEAN-IN-ACTION'[1] AND 'THE GREAT LEARNING'[2] AND OURSELVES TO-DAY

In China when two strangers meet they are able, by certain recognized gambits of polite questioning, to find out quite a number of surface facts about each other. Thus Mr. A of the west may discover that Mr. B of five hundred miles away in the east has connections in his part of the country. By this means conversation flows, and not only with greater interest but also with more intelligence. It would appear that, since the two works here presented in translation were written in one or more of the centuries between the sixth and first B.C., there is need for some such introduction between these authors and their western readers: that is, if the meeting is to evoke interest and any sort of intelligent response. This last is not easy, for China is still very remote to even highly educated people here. Also, when the word 'philosophy' is added to the word 'Chinese,' the more normal Anglo-Saxon mind goes dumb; although there is to be found an escapist kind of person who feels that in the calm atmosphere of ancient Chinese philosophy

---

[1] This work is commonly known among English-speaking people as *The Doctrine of the Mean*. This is open to objection: the Chinese title is *Chung Yung*; *chung* meaning 'centrality,' *yung* meaning 'commonly and generally active.' To translate *chung* as if the centrality conceived were via the image of a bull's-eye in a target is attractive but probably wrong. A mean of truth between exaggerations of error represents more what the author had in mind. To translate *yung* as 'functioning' also is attractive, but it is doubtful whether the author had the biologist's notion of functioning. I have, therefore, given the book's English name as *The Mean-in-action*.

The Ch'eng-Chu School of the Sung dynasty made *The Great Learning* the first of the Four Books, and *The Mean-in-action* the second. Normally, in writing, I put them in the reverse order, the reason for this is that I regard *The Mean-in-action* as the earlier work.

[2] This is the commonly known title of this work. There is much controversy as to what the character represented by 'great' signifies. My own view is that the two words *ta* and *hsüeh* mean the 'learning of greatness.' But 'great learning' trips off the tongue, so it may well stand.

he can project himself into the restful peace which he craves. *The Mean-in-action* and *The Great Learning*, however, were written in very critical times and the authors were not escapists. If there is a calmness about these books it is the calmness to be found in men who have been tested and have reached a new and deeper conviction that the moral order of the universe is supreme.

A natural, and, indeed, a rational, appetite has, therefore, to be excited for what these books have to say. In order to excite this appetite this introduction with its four chapters begins with '*The Mean-in-action* and *The Great Learning* and Ourselves To-day.' Evidence is given to show that in the seventeenth and eighteenth centuries Confucianist thought entered into the main stream of western European thought, influencing some of the most forward-looking minds. Faced as we are with grave perplexities about the nature of our modern civilization, we need to explore this matter further: the more so because the new ideas which came to birth in the eighteenth century are at the heart of the conflict in which Germany and Britain, together with America, are engaged. The second chapter digs deeper into the mine of the past. Cultures and civilizations change out of all knowledge down the centuries. We appreciate this in our own European culture: we have also to appreciate it in Chinese culture. The main changes that came there between the second and the twelfth century are, therefore, set forth; and they are illustrated, as the historian knows there is full warrant for doing, by the Sung thinkers' rediscovery of *The Mean-in-action* and *The Great Learning*. The most influential of these thinkers, Chu Hsi, exalted Reason above Nature (an attitude to life which is the basis of an accusation made against France and England by some of the best thinkers in pre-Nazi Germany). The third chapter goes back to the society which produced our two books. That society was fast breaking away from its ancient moorings. *The Mean-in-action* and *The Great Learning* were formative influences, inspiring men to go out to meet the future. In the final chapter the scholars' questions of date and authorship are considered, and thus the reader is brought face to face, as far as is possible, with the authors, these men who thought that they had the saving truth for their fellows.

Whether this saving truth about man and his place in the universe has anything much to do with us here and now is a matter on which the reader will come to his own decision. I commend: I do not dogmatize. It is, however, permissible to make two remarks. One is that in the third century B.C. violent interstate warfare resulted in the First Emperor setting up a totalitarian regime. All China had to go Nazi. Those who did not were either buried alive or sent to the work-camps at the Great Wall, where most of them died. In *The Mean-in-action* there is a section showing the mind of one earnest individual of Confucianist habits of thought who was attracted by Nazi efficiency. The rest of the book and *The Great Learning* show the mind which brought down that regime and discredited it for ever after. The other remark is that there are a number of influential people in China to-day who believe in the principles of these two books, which, it should be remembered were, before the revolution in education thirty years ago, learnt by heart by every Chinese schoolboy. For example, in the war now raging Chinese power to resist was, on the surface, irretrievably weakened, first by the loss of Shanghai and Nanking, and then by the loss of Hankow. A few days before Hankow fell Marshal Chiang called a mass meeting of the civil officials.[1] He opened the proceedings by drawing attention to the fact that it was a cold day, and since the soldiers at the front were mostly without overcoats, it would be appropriate if those assembled removed theirs. They did. The nation's leader then said that he had called them together to face certain facts in the situation. The first was that those who wanted peace in the world had to see to it that their

[1] The details of this meeting were recounted to me by one of the officials present. Enemy planes roared overhead while the generalissimo was speaking, and, from time to time, he had to wait before he could make himself heard. No one moved during the silences.

country was well governed. Those who aimed at that had to see to it that harmony reigned in the family group. Those who aimed at that had to see to it that they made men of themselves. Having enunciated this primary fact the leader went on to deal with the evacuation of the capital and a continuance of the resistance. His statement of principle was taken word for word from the opening sentences of *The Great Learning*; and, when he and his armies retired further west, the officials he had exhorted, along with some tens of millions of the people, went with him. To live under Japanese rule was not compatible with making a man of oneself.

How the Contact was made between Confucianism and Europe

It seems a far cry from ancient China to modern Europe, yet on my shelves here in Oxford stands a quarto volume, its stout vellum cover ripped across and its opening pages torn. It is a copy of *Confucius, Sinarum Philosophus, sive Scientia Sinensis*, published in Paris in 1687,[1] the authors being Intorcetta, Herdtrich, Rougement, and Couplet, Jesuit missionaries in China. This battered volume came out of the library of a Scottish Presbyterian minister in whose family its possession can be traced for nearly a hundred years. If only a book could speak and tell us of the hands through which it passed! Did this one by any chance suffer this mishandling in 1793, the year in which the authorities in their panic searched all the bookshops for literature from France, and raided the Scottish Reformers' Convention in Edinburgh? Did Margarot or Sinclair, the delegates from London, take the book with them when they went to the convention, only to be arrested and sent to Botany Bay?

This is conjecture, though strictly within the bounds of possibility. We are, however, in the realm of fact when we note that this *Confucius, Sinarum Philosophus* was read all

[1] Intorcetta had his translation of the *Chung Yung* published in Paris in 1673.

over western Europe, in Italy and Spain—perhaps not in Portugal, for they did not love the Jesuits there—in France, Belgium, Holland, and in England. Wherever there were men of learning ('the Learned,' as they were called) they were, for the most part, eager to get information about this amazing country at the other end of the world which was claimed to have a civilization at least equal to that of Europe with a history almost double the length. Here was the authoritative work, written by men who had spent most of their lives in China, knew the language, and had studied the ancient Scriptures and what the Scholars had to say in interpreting them. The main contents of the book were translations of the '*Ta Hio*' (*Great Learning*), the '*Chum Yum*' (*Mean-in-action*), and the '*Lun Yü*' (*Analects*, discussions and sayings by Confucius and his disciples), three of the four books which the Chinese had come to regard as embodying the essence of the great Confucian tradition. The book also contained a biography of Confucius and a chronological table beginning at 2697 B.C., and had an introduction of 115 pages.

This, too, was full of meat for 'the Learned,' for it not only gave a short historical account of the philosophical sects and religions in China, but also set forth the grounds of the Jesuit conviction about the Scholars' religion. This, as their revered Matteo Ricci had led them to believe, was that Confucianism was to all intents and purposes a worship of the True God, sharply to be distinguished from the idolatries of the common people.

Confucius, Sinarum Philosophus was not the only work of its kind. For instance, in 1711 another Jesuit published the three classics which Intorcetta and his friends had introduced to the West and added on a first translation of *Menzius* (*Mencius*), the fourth of the 'Four Books,' and of two other classics, the one on filial piety and the one used in teaching very young children. More popular books also were prepared, written for the most part in French, giving the gist of the Confucianist ethic and political precepts. And, on the other hand, the Jesuits' enemies, the

Portuguese missionary and trading interests, and conservative people who revolted against this exaltation of an alien culture, saw to it that the public were primed about the bad half of the Chinese picture.

Two Contrasted Opinions on China

It were well to quote here two men whose names are hardly known to-day, but who in their age achieved a very considerable reputation: one a mathematician and astronomer; the other an Arabist, both of them priests. Louis Le Comte, a Jesuit and mathematician to Louis XIV, was sent by him to the Emperor of China with a present of astronomical instruments. He stayed in China ten years, travelling widely, and on his return published *Mémoires et Remarques* (Paris, 1696). What he thought is shown by the following:

In fine, his [Confucius's] gravity and mildness in the use of the world, his rigorous abstinence—for he passed for the soberest man of the empire—his contempt of the good things of the world, that continual attention and watchfulness over his actions, and then—which we find not among the sages of antiquity—his humility and modesty would make a man apt to judge that he was not a mere philosopher formed by reason, but a man inspired by God for the reformation of this new world. (English translation, 1738, p. 199.)[1]

However it be, that God had made his wide distribution of grace, I am sure of all nations China has least reason to complain, since no one has received a larger portion than she. (Ibid., p. 323.)

It may surprise us that the man who could write like this was at the same time a fervent evangelizer. What will not surprise us is that he was condemned by the Faculty of Theology in Paris for holding such convictions, particularly for maintaining that for two thousand years [2] 'the Chinese had the knowledge of the true God, and have practised

[1] First English translation, 1697. Three translations in Germany in 1699 and 1700, two in Holland in 1698 and 1710. Cp. Cordier, *Bibliotheca Sinica*.
[2] This refers to 2,000 years before Christ. The Jesuit Fathers accepted Chinese tradition that their culture took civilized shape in the third millennium B.C.

the most pure morality, while Europe and almost all the whole world wallowed in error and corruption.'

The other writer, Eusebius Renaudot, had an entirely different view of China. He purposely translated from the Arabic two Mohammedan accounts from the ninth century of visits to China and wrote a *Dissertation on the Chinese Learning* (Paris, 1718) in order that he might explode this bubble of admiration. He says of Chinese ritual:

We need only examine into the nature of these ceremonies to be convinced that those who could imagine them in the least analogous with Virtue, had not the least idea of Moral Virtues. . . . They are the Science of a Gentleman-usher, or some such officer, not of a Philosopher. (English translation, 1733, p.234.)

Père Renaudot clearly can apply the lash with his tongue. Listen to this:

What we are taught by Jesus Christ is too well grounded to want the concurrence of the Chinese Philosophy; and if any believe it may perfect the Mind, and reform the Manners, though they know nothing thereof but by Paraphrases as obscure as the Text; they are to be advised to inquire into what may be objected to the Antiquity of this proud Nation, to their History and their Philosophy. (Ibid. p. xxxvii.)

The significant thing is that he regards himself as going against the fashion of his day:

As for the Chinese Learning, we have exposed ourselves to great Contradiction, many of the Learned having a long while been of quite a contrary opinion, though not a soul of them could be an immediate Judge of what he advanced, ignorant of that dreadful tongue which requires no less than the Life of Man to be duly attained. The Missionaries, indeed, thought they might safely make the Chinese Philosophers instrumental towards the conversion of the whole Nation, and their view was laudable enough; but others, and especially Libertines, have strangely perverted the excessive things which have been reported of the Chinese Antiquities; and have assumed them as a Weapon wherewith to attack the Authority of Scripture and its Superstructure, the Christian Religion; as also the Universality of the Flood, and to maintain that the World is much older than it is thought to be. . . . Ignorant people, such as the Author of the Preadamite System, are apt to believe whatever flatters their own Conceptions. (Ibid. p. xxxvi.)

The Discovery of a New Earth

There can be no question but that feeling ran very high over China. Were the Jesuits right in what they reported? If they were, then for the religious and theological mind the revelation of God, which the Scholastics had taught so convincingly was above ordinary reason, was not confined to the 'Scripture and its superstructure, the Christian religion'; for the classicist, with the convictions born of the Renaissance, here was another treasure house of wisdom of yet greater antiquity than Greece and Rome; for the man who was concerned about manners and customs and the ruling of states, in China, perhaps, was to be found the solution of the problems which were pressing on his Europe. Thus, behind the emotional tension of controversy lay questions of fundamental principles, and these not old, dead issues which to-day we may rightly forget. Modern Europe was being born, and modern America, and the ideas which became alive in our ancestors two hundred years back are the very ideas which make the war of 1940 one of extermination.

To understand the controversies which raged, particularly in France and Germany, we must go back to the fifteenth and sixteenth centuries, when a new spirit of adventure stirred in the kings of Spain and Portugal and their mariner subjects, just about the same time that the same spirit stirred in the Ming Court in China, and sent its mariners exploring to the coast of Africa. Before the eastern oceans had been penetrated China figured in people's imagination. The Middle Ages had known about a mysterious great country beyond the Caucasus and the deserts and mountains of central Asia. Then had come Marco Polo's thrilling story and the stories of the Franciscan missionaries about 'Cambaluc and Far Cathay.' China was not fantastic in the way in which the legends had made out, with their Anthropophagi and other marvels, but none the less gorgeous with the pageantry of its courts, to be marvelled at for the vast unity of its sway, and, above all, rich beyond the dreams of avarice. When, therefore, Columbus set out across the Atlantic and ran into America, he was looking for a quicker and easier route to China. Other navigators were more successful than Columbus; and so by the beginning of the seventeenth century there had begun that stream of trading ships across the world which were to bring more and more information about an actual China. The more people heard the more their curiosity was aroused, the more they wanted to hear about its history and cultural traditions. Hence every three to five years a new book on China was published somewhere, beginning with Gonzalez de Mendoza's bulky volumes in 1585.[1] The significant thing is that if a book was published in Italy, Spain, Portugal, France, Holland, Germany, or wherever it might be, the chances were that in a very few years an edition or a translation of it would appear in more than one of the other countries.

It was a 'New World' which impinged on people's settled notions and started revolutionizing them, the more so since parts of that world had civilizations which went far back in history. Of course, China was not the only country which excited new speculations about life. There was Turkey, and India, and more particularly Persia, with its austere Zoroastrian cult, not to speak of Mexico and Peru and the 'savages' of Africa and North America. But for certain special reasons China was the most impressive and unsettling of them all. No other country was so open to missionary evangelism, or had so large and influential a body of missionaries as that which the Jesuit Order placed there. These men were specially selected and trained for their task. They were, beside being evangelists, also scientists, historians, students of politics and manners and customs, explorers and map makers, and, above all, men who

---

[1] Cordier's *Bibliotheca Sinica* notes some twenty editions of this work in Rome, Paris, London, etc.

gave themselves to the study of Chinese literature and the sympathetic understanding of Chinese ways of thinking. It was the policy of the Order, in China as in the countries of Europe where its Fathers had been the heart and soul of the Counter-Reformation, to understand the society in which it lived, make itself useful to those in authority, and so achieve political prestige and be in a position to bring the world under the rule of Christ and His vicar, the pope. In the second place, when these devoted students, Ricci, Le Bouvet and Noël, Intorcetta, and their fellows, came to grips with the different systems of Chinese thought, religious and otherwise, they found, on the one hand, that Taoism and Buddhism were alien and profoundly offensive to them; on the other hand, that the Confucianist scholars in many ways talked the same language, and their ancient scriptures contained much which was either expressly in relation to the worship of a High God or directed to the culture of a noble virtue. It was, therefore, with the thrill of a notable discovery that they set themselves to convince the heads of the Order at home and, when they were denounced by the Dominicans and Franciscans, to appeal to the religious intelligence of all learned Catholics. They wrote books and sent scholarly converts to Europe in order that men might judge for themselves. Thus, whatever might be the case with other parts of the 'New World,' it was brought home to liberal minds that the best of Chinese philosophy and religion was not alien to their 'Great Tradition,' that at bottom it affirmed the same simple verities, and, therefore, was in no sense exotic.

The Discovery of a 'New Heaven'

Ricci, Schall, Verbiest, and their fellow scientists in the China mission are significant for another reason, namely that they had imbibed the new knowledge (*scientia*) which, by the end of the seventeenth century, was making the Scholastics' philosophy of God and Nature vastly open to doubt. Galileo was followed by Newton, and he succeeded in drawing the various threads together and making 'the first physical synthesis.' It was a matter of calculation. Behold the universe, proved one and indivisible, not by inference from the existence of Almighty God, but on the basis of inerrant mathematics. Behold Nature, the same in the heavens as in the earth, containing no place for miracle, its laws ascertained by processes of reason and not by acts of faith. We can see, stage by stage, the development of this new mind which has been regarded as the chief characteristic of modern man. One of its main interim achievements was a reavowal of belief in the existence of God; for the earlier Nature philosophers, for the most part, did not disavow the existence of God: rather they discovered in Him, in a sense very different from St. Thomas Aquinas, the God of Nature, the Nature which they were so busy exploring. He was, too, the God of Reason. Reason was His perfect gift to man.

When we speak of the Nature philosophers we have to include Catholic priests and Protestant clergymen as well as the laymen who had been educated in a Catholic or Protestant environment: some of them satisfied with Church and State, some of them not: some of them working very much alone, stoking the engine of their thought with their own fuel, others meeting for discussion and carrying on prodigious correspondence with their fellow philosophers. Both in their letters and in their published works we are again and again in doubt whether they are considering religion from a philosophical angle or philosophy from a religious angle. In any case, there was a highly significant term in the current coin of their talk, 'Natural Religion,' of which the two chief examples for them were the Stoicism of the ancient Romans and the Confucianism of the contemporary Chinese scholars. Whatever of traditional Christianity might have to be discarded in the light of the 'New Heaven' and the 'New Earth,' there was this indestructible residuum which reason could be counted on to support. Being satisfied on this score, some of the philosophers found themselves driven on to consider what was the relation between religion and politics. There was the question which proved so provocative: What was the ultimate foundation of authority in the State?

The New Philosophy and 'The Great Learning' and 'The Mean-in-action'

There are four thinkers who stand out in the generations following Francis Bacon as formative influences and as representative of the new critical spirit in philosophy. Of these four, Descartes, Spinoza,[1] Leibniz, and Locke, the first two lived a little too early to be affected by more than what may be described as the fact of China, that is the great State and civilization of China. Of the other two, Leibniz claims our chief attention, for in Locke's literary remains there is evidence that he was fully aware of the fact of China, but not as far as I have been able to discover of anything more. Leibniz, on the contrary, from his early twenties to the last of his seventy years had a passion for information on China, and took every opportunity he had of forgathering with the Jesuit missionaries. What precisely the effect on him was, this, as we shall see, is not easy to define: it is enough here to say that there are some particularly close resemblances between Leibniz's special theories and what he could find in *Confucius, Sinarum Philosophus*. That he read this in the year in which it was published we know from a letter of that year; as also we know from his correspondence with Arnauld that it was between 1686 and 1690 that his ideas about 'simple substance' and the pre-established harmony in the universe took shape.

It were as well for the reader, however, that he should approach this genesis of the modern mind from a more general angle. Let us take the words which not only Leibniz, but many other inquiring minds, were reading after 1687: the sentences which are the beginning of *The Great*

---

[1] At first I thought that Professor Chu went a great deal further than I could in tracing Chinese influence in Descartes's and Spinoza's systems of thought. In the last resort, however, he qualifies—I gather for the time being—his more general affirmation by the statement that concrete evidence is hard to find.

Learning and *The Mean-in-action* as they appeared in *Confucius, Sinarum Philosophus*:

Magnum adeoque virorum Principum, sciendi institutum consistit in expoliendo, seu excolendo rationalem naturam a coelo inditam; ut scilicet haec, ceu limpidissimum speculum, abstersis pravorum appetituum maculis, ad pristinam claritatem suam redire possit. Consistit deinde in renovando seu reparando populum, suo ipsius scilicet exemplo & adhortatione. Consistit demum in sistendo firmiter, seu perseverando in summo bono: per quod hic Interpretes intelligi volunt summam actionum omnium cum recta ratione conformitatem.[1]

And then a few lines further down, a continuation of that logical ethical sequence to which Marshal Chiang drew the attention of his officers:

Jam vero volentes recte componere suum corpus, seu externum totius personae habitum, prius rectificabant suum animum . . . volentes autem rectificare suum animum, prius rectificabant . . . suam intentionem. . . . Ad summun apicem perducere vim intellectivam, consistit in penetrando res omnes, seu rerum omnium rationes.

From *The Mean-in-action*:

Id quod a caelo est homini inditum dicitur natura rationalis: quod huic conformatur natura, eam consequitur, dicitur regula & seu consentaneum rationi, restaurare quoad exercitium hanc regulam se suaque per eam moderando, dicitur institutio, seu disciplina virtutum.

Mark those expressions, 'the rational nature of man imposed by Heaven is conformed to nature' (i.e. the nature of men and the nature of things), 'agreement with reason,' and, above all, 'to lead on the power of the intellect to the highest apex consists in penetrating all things,' or the *rationes* (structural laws) of all things. That was precisely what these Nature philosophers in western Europe were set to do. They had also a holy passion for *limpidissimum speculum*

---

[1] My English translation of these and the following two passages will be found not to correspond in every particular with the Latin here. Also the Latinist will discover that the learned author gives alternative renderings. This is one of the significant features of this Intorcetta-Couplet book.

and were in no way discouraged when one thinker after another had his limpid speculation contested and surpassed by other speculations apparently yet more limpid. It is their immense courage and pertinacity which we have to admire in these men who broke new ground in every region of the conscious reasoning mind. Each of them was intensely himself, exploring his very self, as it seemed to him. And he was the more aware of his self and had the greater confidence in it, because he was exploring the nature of things and his relation to them, and by this means, by the path of perfecting knowledge, he was opening the way to the perfection of virtue, i.e. *recte componere suum corpus*.

The Question as to the Nature and Extent of Confucianist Influence

To the student of eighteenth-century literature these concepts have the authentic ring of his period. To the ordinary, moderately well-educated man to-day, at any rate, in the democratic countries, they may sound a little pompous; but, after all, they are what most people take for granted in 'science and common sense.' To the historian they are matter for investigation because they plainly came to the philosophizers of those days as something new, as discoveries which liberated the mind of man. To us at this point in the story of this chapter the question is whether Confucianist philosophy was in any real sense responsible, or partly responsible, for these discoveries. A vastly important question, for it is the particular modern product, a combination of Rationalism and Humanism, which emerges to view, and there are a number of resonant voices telling us that Europe took the wrong turning in the eighteenth century, hence the present sanguinary impasse.

That China, and more particularly late Confucianist philosophy, had something to do with the emergence of this type of mind is, I think, an inescapable conclusion. In that philosophy is found the same combination of Rationalism and Humanism, the same exaltation of Nature and Reason. Along with this there is the same faith in man as by nature good and by nature rational, as needing only knowledge to be added to his aptitude for goodness for his virtue to become perfect, and for him to achieve a perfect society adapted to his disciplined desire and educated capacity for happiness. Here, therefore, is a peculiarly precise time sequence, first of interest in China and wide-spread surface knowledge of her, and then of those distinctive emphases in metaphysics, ethics, and political and social science.

If that be the nature of the influence, what of the extent? The clue here is to be found in the famous French movement known as the Enlightenment, the movement from which came the Revolution. The leading spirits in this movement, Voltaire, Diderot, Helvétius, Baron d'Holbach, Montesquieu, had this distinguishing feature, that they all believed in the sovereignty of reason with a naïveté which is almost incredible to us to-day. To them the age of reason was on the threshold, and—to put it somewhat crudely—if only they could get their great *Encyclopédie* published, this comprehensive mass of exact information as to the world of Nature and the world of Man would open every one's eyes to the nature of true happiness for the individual and for society as a whole. All the long-established tyrannies and ingrained vices would disappear: man, rational man, would be master of his fate.

The value of this clue lies in the way it shows the limit of direct Chinese influence as well as its extent. These Encyclopaedists differed widely in their appreciation both of the fact of China and of its philosophy. To Voltaire, the most widely read author in western Europe, they were a continual source of inspiration, and it is unquestionable that, much as he admired England, he admired China more. In Confucianism, the 'Scholars' Religion,' as the Jesuit Fathers had taught him to call it, he saw the living archtype of that 'Natural Religion' to which reason called all men to give their allegiance. As a satirist, as a man of imagination, as a serious historian, in his long list of plays, stories, poems, his dictionary of philosophy, and his final essay on customs among the nations of the world, the influence of China is plainly visible. And yet, when it came to the humanist witness against the hideous abuses of aristocratic privilege, he did not show the instinct of compassion which figured so in the Confucianist ethic.

At the other extreme stand Helvétius and d'Holbach, the one very much under the influence of the extremer form of British Deism, the other the slave of physical science, imbued with the cynicism of ultra-rationalism. Both of them in their published works show that they did not share Voltaire's enthusiasm for China. They were hard-headed men, and yet in their hard-headed way they reveal, particularly d'Holbach in his *Système Social*, the beginnings of the new humanitarian conscience which became so marked a feature of the new philosophy and of contemporary Catholicism and Protestantism. But Diderot, standing midway between the two extremes, is the most illuminating to us of those devotees of Enlightenment. He was in so many ways the very pattern of a Neo-Confucianist scholar: learned and viewing Nature as a pure intellectualist, tolerant with the tolerance of a man who is wedded to principle and, at the same time, convinced that intellectual man must work together; incredibly patient and long-suffering, and with it all naïvely optimistic over the essential goodness of man and his capacity for obeying reason. And it was this Diderot who had the profoundest admiration for Leibniz: Leibniz, the most speculative of metaphysicians and the most devoted among 'the Learned' to 'practical philosophy,' in which sphere, he said, 'I almost think it is necessary that Chinese missionaries should be sent to us to teach us the aim and practice of natural theology, as we send missionaries to them to instruct them in revealed theology.'[1]

This must suffice for the main stream of the Enlightenment movement. Our clue brings us thus far: that in those exciting mid-century days in Paris the Confucianist influence must be taken as a double one; on the one hand, a definite one, recognized as pointing men to a more rational, more humane way of living and thinking with Nature as the benign controller of human destiny; on the

[1] *Novissima Sinica*, quoted by Reichwein, *China and Europe*. London, 1925, p. 80.

other hand, a general pervasive influence along these lines, not recognized as emanating from China because on the face of it, these ideas were so incontestably right, and so the common property of intelligent men all over the world. Those who consciously welcomed this philosophy as Chinese were comparatively few. The majority made no intensive study of it, were content to turn over the leaves of the missionary tomes,[1] perhaps read the more popular works along with a dozen other works which formed the subject of conversation in the *salons* where the Enlightenment enlightened itself. The very fact that this philosophy was not regarded as exotic but as natural, the reasonable one, made it more easily acceptable without consciousness of its source.

To students who would trace out the rich variety of this influence Reichwein's *China and Europe* [2] affords an excellent starting-point. A highly significant series of names will be found there; for example, Wolff, Professor of Theology at Halle, exiled in 1721 because of a lecture he gave in praise of Chinese philosophy, and Dr. Quesnay, who worked to make Louis XVI a Chinese sage-emperor and France a state run on Chinese economic principles. But for detailed examination I have selected, as outstanding examples of the conscious and unconscious influence, Leibniz and Rousseau; for it was through their minds more than any one else's that Confucianist philosophy came as far as it did into European thought. The interesting thing is that this brilliant speculative philosopher and this ardent Romantic were, in contrast to the tendencies of their age, stubborn theists. That is to say, each in his own way was profoundly convinced that 'God' was a living reality, ever active, ever-present, the Supreme Person. Both of them were awake to the sick condition of religion in western Christendom. Along with their deist and atheist

---

[1] In Du Halde's *The General History of China*, Paris, 1735, a list of twenty-seven Jesuit works is given as the sources from which he drew.

[2] This work contains the best account I know of the widespread enthusiasm for Chinese art and the profound influence it exercised in Europe. It is admirable also on the Physiocrats and Goethe. But I find the treatment of Leibniz and Rousseau not so satisfactory.

contemporaries they gloried in the arduous obligation of intellectual liberty and served in the school of reason. But they would not submit either to a theology of retreat or to an agnostic philosophy. In this way they were the most remarkable men of their day.

Leibniz, the Philosopher of the Contingent

Wilhelm Gottfried Leibniz (1646–1716) was a philosopher, if ever there was one. He was ceaselessly speculating about everything in heaven and earth and above and below them; and, whilst he was more learned than any man of his day, he carried his encyclopaedic knowledge lightly. With regard to that knowledge, it is important to remember that he started life under Protestant influences, as a small boy was set to learn Luther's Catechism; and, although throughout his life he was very intimate with Catholic thinkers, and was pressed to enter the Catholic Church, he did not do so. In his teens he was put through the mill of scholastic philosophy; but his mind went away from such studies. He went on to jurisprudence, and then to mathematics, and from these to the close study of the Christian Fathers. From all this he emerged a mathematician rather than a classicist, a dogmatic philosopher with a strong sense of world history, not a Christian apologist bent on bringing any theological tradition up to date.

It was during the acquisitive years of his life that Leibniz came to Chinese philosophy. As has already been stated, his correspondence shows that he gave his mind to it. In fact, China became a major interest of his life, and for more than forty years he studied and did all he could to stir up his world to an interest in the Chinese and their philosophy. As for his knowledge of Confucianism, he relied not only on published works. He was also in correspondence with some of the Jesuit missionaries.[1] There is, indeed, amongst

[1] Owing to the outbreak of war in September 1939 I have been unable to follow up this line of inquiry as I proposed to do. There is a considerable quantity of relevant material tucked away in libraries in Germany, particularly the one at Hanover.

his biographical material a whole battery of accumulative evidence demonstrating his sustained interest in that philosophy and admiration of it along certain lines. On the other hand, when we examine his main philosophical works, we find hardly a reference to it; and, as if this were not intriguing enough, there is the fact that in those same works, in the metaphysical as well as the ethical, the position he takes up is, with but a single exception, one with which a good Neo-Confucianist would have found himself in substantial agreement. The exception is important, because it is that very affirmation of the existence of a Living God which Leibniz made with such peculiar emphasis. Even so, considering the intricate convolutions of Leibniz's theories, and the equal intricacy of Neo-Confucianist thought, the resemblances are such that they cannot be dismissed as meaningless.[1] So also with his latest works, in the *Monadology* and *Principles of Nature and Grace Founded on Reason*, the most remarkable similarities occur. To read Chu Hsi's commentary on *The Mean - in - action* is to find Leibniz's distinctive ideas staring one in the face. And then—to complete the chain—to go on and read *Confucius, Sinarum Philosophus* is to discover that the translators mixed in the Neo-Confucianist interpretations with the original text, so that when Leibniz read this work he was actually imbibing Confucianism very largely through the Sung adaptation of it.

The situation thus revealed is one with very far-reaching implications into which it is impossible to go here. It must suffice to point out that, in spite of the Confucianists' worship of *T'ien* (Heaven), and their general haziness as to personality in God it is a mistake to suppose that Confucianism generally as a religious philosophy is deistic in essence. The eighteenth-century Deists (with Jesuits among them) may have hailed the 'Scholars' Religion' as a useful corroboration of their theories about 'Natural Religion,' but 'Nature' in classical Confucianism, and even in Neo-Confucianism, is not a wholly mechanical chain of cause and effect, but something living in the fullest sense, characterized

[1] Cp. Appendix I on Leibniz and Chu Hsi.

by what Leibniz called 'the contingent' as well as 'the necessary': 'the contingent,' that range of possibilities, as distinct from actualities on the one hand and improbabilities on the other, which goes along with the reality of the individual and the personal. In this respect, as in some other very vital respects, Leibniz was a good Confucianist as well as a good Christian.

The natural inference, and I think, within limits, the right one, is that the Chinese influence went very deep in him, deeper than he knew, since the spirit of the man was such that he gladly and easily accepted what he read in the Jesuit books. He was a Humanist and a Rationalist as well as a Theist, his mind very likely working along the same lines before these ideas came to meet him from outside. But the major explanation of his silence may well lie in the fact that in the long and bitter struggle between the Jesuits and their enemies over Chinese religion, it was the Jesuits who were beaten. In 1704 the pope [1] and the Inquisition decided finally that the Scholars' Religion was not akin to the religion of revelation, and thereafter China was suspect in religious circles. With regard to the limits, they can be stated quite clearly in broad outline. Leibniz came to the conclusion that in 'the theoretical and philosophical sciences (mathematics,[1] astronomy, logic, metaphysics) Europe had gone farther than China': a view the truth of which cannot be questioned except in relation to metaphysics. But Leibniz, with his belief in the Christian revelation, would not question the metaphysical superiority. Besides, we may suspect that he found the Jesuit works not only suggestive but also puzzling. The Latin of *Confucius, Sinarum Philosophus* is cumbrous and involved: so that there was good grounds for Renaudot's gibe: 'Paraphrases as obscure as the text.' *Limpidissimum speculum*

---

[1] Professor Chu has impressive data to advance, particularly a letter from Leibniz to Le Bouvet in which he refers to assistance he derived from material supplied by Le Bouvet dealing with Shao Kang-chieh's treatment of the sixty-four symbols in the *Classic of Changes*. The inference is that Leibniz owed his inspiration for his *Arithmétique Binaire* to this quarter.

sounded very well; but what if the grammar and syntax of the translator was anything but limpid?¹

On the other hand, Leibniz was convinced that Europe had much to learn from China in 'practical philosophy.' Here, again, to read *The Great Learning* is to find oneself in the ethical and political world of ideals into which Leibniz's reason carried him. In brief, familiar as he was with Roman jurisprudence and the recent expositions of 'Natural Law,' his mind, nevertheless, cut right through the issues which occupied the minds of his contemporaries. He was concerned with the individual, not as an individual possessor of 'natural rights,' but as the possessor of natural obligations. It was the duty of man to see that other people got their rights, and this applied to prince as well as to pauper. Rulers, in the last resort, had no rights except those which came to them naturally from governing for the good of all; and by 'good' Leibniz meant 'the greatest possible happiness of all.' He did not think so much in terms of the nationalist state of his day but of 'the totality (*assemblage*) of all spirits.' Finally, effectual virtue is a combination of goodness in action and knowledge (wisdom). With these combined man achieves happiness, the happiness of perfection which is the goal of the 'commonwealth of the universe.' All this is high Confucianism of the kind which Leibniz read about in *The Mean-in-action* and *The Great Learning*.

Thus Leibniz, the only man of his time who had a competent philosophy of the spirit to set against the compromises of the Deists and the Utilitarians. Some of my readers may protest and urge that all he emphasized can be found in the Great Tradition of Europe, or at any rate, may be taken as the natural outcome of it. True, there are all sorts of parallels. In the case of so learned a man it could hardly be otherwise. But the protestor must

¹ Père François Noël's translation, published in Prague in 1711, is much more readable, but I have no evidence that Leibniz ever read it. On general grounds it is difficult to believe that he did not, for, by 1711, although he was well on in his sixties, his interest in China was no less eager than in earlier years.

B

remember that we are dealing with a very singular, for Leibniz's age unique, combination of ideas in metaphysics, ethics, and political philosophy. There is no natural outcome in the sense of being inevitable about such a combination. And further, in considering a problem of this sort, we have to beware in the West, even to-day, of the prejudices which go along with the dogged presupposition that our civilization is the only true one and, apart from the revolutionary influence of a Jewish sect in classical times, has developed in unilinear fashion all down the ages. When this view of our cultural history was based on a religious foundation alone, there was a certain logicality about it, provided, of course, it was self-evident, not only that the Christian revelation was unique, but also that organized Christianity was spiritually in apostolic succession, and its culture and civilization was a unity of an adequately representative Christian character. The very strong tendency, however, has been not to base this view on religion alone, but to include the idea that we were the sole legatees of the uniquely precious culture of Greece and Rome. That that culture is precious to the world we may confidently believe, but not that it is unique in the sense of being the necessary foundation of a premier civilization. It is hardly necessary to add that the idea of a premier civilization includes the idea of the right to dominance; there was further the notion that the people of the Atlantic seaboard had an innate genius for governing the world, an argument which Adolf Hitler and his Nazis have now adapted so that it applies to the German people.

Rousseau, the Prophet of the 'General Will'

We turn now to Rousseau, about whose political philosophy the western world has been arguing ever since. To begin with, he became the saint of the French Revolution, for he did more than any other man to bring together the three constituent parts of its passionate creed, Liberty, Equality, and Fraternity. And yet, if he had lived to see it, he would surely have revolted against it, as Wordsworth did. The 'blood bath' might be Reason, but it was not Nature, the tender Mother Nature whom the two men adored. That, as every one knows, is the position to which Rousseau finally came, that Nature was opposed to Reason, with the result that to-day he can be regarded as an apostle by two fiercely hostile camps, the one fighting for universal, equalitarian democracy, the other fighting for totalitarianism and *Kultur*.

Again, we have to face the emergence of new, immensely influential ideas in an old, deeply rooted, and very varied culture, and the question is whether the new can be adequately explained in terms of the old. This time let us pay particular attention to the Renaissance, for that is part of the unilinear explanation; and it is taken for granted that the new classical studies not only could, but actually did, continue as a vivifying influence right through into the eighteenth century. I should have thought that the precise opposite was fairly certain. Certainly Locke and Leibniz were not inspired by their university studies in the classics; and in so far as they used 'the ancients' in their speculations, it was as a check, and, when they came to write, as a means of commending their theories to more slow-moving minds. The classical appeal was to authority rather than to reason, as can be seen in Wollaston's *Religion of Nature*. He is a typical classicist of that epoch, clear, precise, pithy, having something to say and saying it, but ingrainedly conservative, besotted with his masses of proof-texts. But the chief example is to be found in the studies of Natural Law and the theory of society which engrossed so many of the most learned minds from the sixteenth to the eighteenth century. Significant studies, yes; but how incredibly cautious, arguing interminably 'about it and about'!

The question is what it was that released the spring in Rousseau's mind; and the question must be pressed home. On the one hand, he was a Genevan at a particularly conservative time, learnt his Latin along with his elements of the Christian faith from a pious old Calvinist minister whom he loved, and thus came to manhood deeply imbued with the

Great Tradition. He did not show himself to be what could be called a good Christian, whether as a Protestant or a Catholic, but he was very Christian in his consciousness of God as a living God, and in his sense of sin and the frailty of his nature. With regard to Greece and Rome, they also were immensely real to him. In particular he saw in the early Rome of the Republic a pattern of what social men could achieve. On the other hand, when he came to write *Émile* and *Le Contrat Social*, it is doubly clear that other forces had been working in him. Thus, for example, although the Stoics had insisted that man's rational soul was his distinctive characteristic, that 'the Good' was part of Reason and dependent on it, this was not what Rousseau made of man. Thinkers like Shaftesbury and Hume might follow the classical lead, and thereby see man as good by nature, and Hobbes might make all virtue nothing but enlightened selfishness; but although Rousseau was influenced by them, his ultimate belief about man was very different from theirs. His own bitter experience taught him that Reason made him a slave, whilst Nature at the least set his feet on the path of liberty.

This discovery drove him from Paris, cost him the friendship of the Encyclopaedists, and even made him abandon his hope for fame. He became the solitary wanderer of the Hermitage, in his more active moments the correspondent of young ladies, and the extoller of domestic virtues. But that was not all. The forces working in him and his own *daimon* drove him out into strange new country, and he sat down and wrote the two books which went exactly counter to his Hermitage philosophy and roused all western Europe by the challenge they gave.

'The fundamental dogma of the natural goodness of man finds no place directly in the *Social Contract*; but it lurks behind the whole of his political theory, and is, indeed, throughout, his master conception.' These words, coming from a twentieth-century student of Rousseau,[1] are un-

---

[1] G. H. D. Cole, *The Social Contract and Discourses*. Everyman's Library, No. 660, p. xli.

questionably true, not only in relation to the *Social Contract*. The natural goodness of man is, indeed, a master conception from which flow the most far-reaching consequences in ethics and religion, in politics and education. It also marks one of the major contrasts between the thought and the history of Europe and China. The one believed that man was bad by nature. The other believed that he was good. From the time when, early in the fifth century, Augustine fought the British monk, Pelagius, on this issue, and had beaten him in the councils of the Church, any idea that man could be good by nature was heresy, and any who thought like this had to do so surreptitiously.[1] Classical philosophy, of course, contained a number of other views, notably the Stoic and Epicurean, but after St. Augustine's day the Great Tradition in Europe came to be built on his doctrine. The Reformation, although it sifted so much of Catholic theology, retained the dogma of badness; and Calvin, to be sure, the man who did so much to make Rousseau's Geneva, carried the argument to the extremity of its logic.

In China it was the exact reverse which happened. In the early days there was the same conflict of opposing views, one that man was by nature bad, another setting forth the nexus of pleasure and pain as Epicurus had done. But by the second century A.D. the theory of goodness had become predominant, and even Buddhism with its counter-philosophy, not to speak of the hard experience of war and civil corruption, was unable to shake Chinese conviction in this. The curious thing is that apparently Confucius had nothing to say on the question. The theory was first advanced a hundred and fifty years after him by Mencius; and Mencius's book was not given a place in the Confucianist canon until the Sung dynasty.

There is a striking coincidence between Mencius's view and Rousseau's. Not only is man credited with this instinct and aptitude for goodness apart from reason, but

[1] Dr. Alex. Souter, the great authority on Pelagian texts, informs me that in medieval writings reproductions of passages from Pelagian works can often be found, but seldom with acknowledgment of source.

Rousseau's main argument is the one which Mencius had used as his main argument. It is that man cannot bear to see his fellow men suffering or in danger. Reason may, on reflection, reveal incentives of self-interest for helping, but the impulse comes first. This applies to men in relation to animals as well as to fellow humans. To nurture the sprouts of goodness in one is to be 'a man,' to let them wither and die is to be less than a man.

Further, since this theory is essentially optimistic, and therefore open to suspicion as entailing an idealized view of man, it is significant that both Mencius and Rousseau are realists in that they pay strict attention to man's senses, and are agreed in making these the root not only of a division of interest, but also of a community of interest. As we may say, through having the same taste for good food a man knows intuitively what it means to his neighbour to go without food. From this springs what in *The Great Learning* is called 'the Way' (Principle of the Measuring Square), namely, what I do not like men doing to me, I do not do to them. Rousseau denounces the idea of complete self-sacrificing altruism as something which simply does not work; and in this shows himself a good Confucianist in contrast to a Mohist, for Mo Ti and his followers were prepared to 'wear the hair off their shins' in their undiscriminating love for all men. That, said the Confucianist, is against man's nature. Not that there was any limit to what the individual might have to suffer and do in following the Great Way of man's common happiness; but that the impulse must come from Nature and then be disciplined and directed by Reason.

When we turn to the theme of *Le Contrat Social*, man in ordered association and the need for government, we find both coincidences and the reverse. The coincidences again are very striking, and again for the reason that Rousseau followed a highly original line. We must confine our attention to the two major points, the 'Social Contract,' the problem which the jurists had been discussing for three centuries, and Rousseau's 'General Will' which the students of political science have been trying to make sense of ever since.

Rousseau saw that the jurists, Bodin, Grotius, Pufendorf, and the others, with their balancing of rights by nature and rights in law could never solve the problem of the Social Contract. Besides, they were ignoring a vital distinction. There is a pact of association when people come together with the aim of achieving a greater happiness for each than can be achieved in independence. If that happiness is not achieved, the pact is automatically void. Quite distinct from that is the pact of government which can only exist on the basis of agreed on 'fundamental laws.' If these—what we usually call the Constitution of a State—are not conducive to the end contemplated by the pact of association and the end of common happiness is not being achieved, then the Executive is not fulfilling the end for which these laws called it into existence, and it automatically ceases to have any standing. If, on the other hand, the Executive in dealing with the endless situations involving private interests, actually increases the area and force of common interest, then all is well. Both the basic pact of association and the subsidiary pact of government hold good. This can only happen because, in addition to the private wills dealing with private interests, there exists a general will dealing with common interests.

Mencius did not think in terms of a deliberate pact of association nor of a legal pact of government; but apart from this Rousseau's argument is exactly that of the Mencius school, particularly after the Sung Dynasty, when a new and more methodical emphasis was laid on the force of private desires. But the most striking thing is the realistic way in which both Rousseau and the Confucianists argued, not from what men might be, but, as the former said in the opening words of *Le Contrat Social*, 'men being taken as they are.' And the same applies to the 'General Will.' The hard conditions and dangers of national life keep it alive, particularly in relation to bad rulers. This makes it infallible, because it is only the common people who really know where the shoe pinches.

Finally, Rousseau was clear, as the Confucianists were before him, that acts of sovereignty must be distinguished from the exercise of executive authority. The one creates spontaneous obedience by its inherent rightness. The other may bring a spontaneous response, but its characteristic is that its commands are backed by force. This theory is not easily understood by the legalist mind, the type of mind which is far more common in the West than in China; and Rousseau, who could argue like a jurist, entered on refinements of explanation which are foreign to Confucianist thinkers. The surprising thing is that he should have got through to the Confucianist conclusion at which he arrived. Thus, for example, he saw that the people could not, out of their poverty of wisdom, achieve the supreme act of sovereignty, the making of wise fundamental laws. An 'initial legislator' of supreme virtue and supreme wisdom is needed, one who 'ought to feel himself capable of changing human nature.' This is distinctly out of line with Rousseau's application of the 'General Will,' but it is entirely in line with the Chinese lore of the Sage Kings, examples of which are to be found in *The Mean-of-action* and *The Great Learning*.

Now does all this mean that Rousseau deliberately, or, at any rate, consciously, moulded his political and ethical thinking on Confucianist lines? Not in the least. In the first place, he quite clearly revolted against the exaggerated admiration of the Chinese which he found in Voltaire and others. In his first Dijon essay he held them up to view as the great modern example of a people who paid honour to learning, and when attacked by 'rude and ignorant barbarians' (i.e. the Tartars) failed to preserve their liberties. 'What advantage has the country reaped from the honours bestowed on its learned men? Can it be that of being peopled by a race of scoundrels and slaves?' About that statement there can be no question; but it hardly represents his considered opinion, for in his 1758 essay on political economy he had some very complimentary things to say about the Chinese system. Speaking generally, his scattered references to China reveal that amount of general knowledge on China which would otherwise have to be assumed on the ground that no man could live, as he did, in the circle of the Enlightenment for thirteen years and not hear China and its philosophy repeatedly discussed. The art of China was displayed in the *salons*, the 'wisdom of China' was in men's mouths,[1] its agricultural economy held up as a model, its history scrutinized in the travellers' and missionaries' books, and even missionaries themselves were to be met with at receptions. All this was part of the great, bewildering pattern of fact and theory which came as a spate of impressions into the acutely impressionable soul of the young citizen from Geneva.

For a western student of Chinese philosophy it is a most intriguing experience to read Rousseau's later works and to find there, again and again, sentiments expressed which might almost have come straight out of some Chinese book. Equally intriguing, and more tangible to lay hold of, is the comparison of Rousseau's solution of the social and economic problems in western Europe with the solution urged by Dr. Quesnay and his group of Physiocrats— 'the Economists,' as Adam Smith called them. On the face of it, with their schemes for getting Louis XV to be the 'Benevolent Monarch' of Confucianist idealism, they were the true converts of China. They certainly took themselves to be so, as they took themselves also to be severely realistic in the highway which they marked out for the attainment of popular liberty. Actually it was Rousseau, the dreamer who became convinced that no king could be the vehicle of the general will of the people, who

---

[1] Du Halde's encyclopaedic work, *The General History of China, including an Exact and Particular Account of their Customs, Manners, Ceremonies, Religion, Arts, and Sciences*, was published in Paris in 1735, six years before Rousseau arrived there. Montesquieu, whom Rousseau admired greatly, relied largely on this work for the information on China which informs his *Esprit des Lois*. Translations of it were made into English, Dutch, German, and Russian.

discovered the keystone of the Confucianist political arch, namely, that man, the ordinary man as he is with his sprouts of goodness, is the final judge of society's order, whether it is good and whether it is bad.

Most intriguing of all is the religious study of this eighteenth-century rationalist, as he is so often regarded. He had what rationalists can only regard as a morbid sense of sin. He was like St. Paul and St. Augustine, one might almost say, through and through: 'for the good that I would do I do not; but the evil which I would not, that I do': this is the repeated strain in his *Confessions*. And certainly he was morbid over other people's sins, the sins of the people who seemed to his touchy egoism to act towards him with wilful malice. Yet, in these later years when he went back to the pious practice of his Protestant training and 'read his Bible every day,' he is found to have discarded the great dogma of Calvinist Christianity. He affirmed the Confucianist dogma: man is good, and that not by Reason but by Nature.

There is more than one way of looking at the development of the mind and soul in this genius. One is that the European tradition was lacking in certain truths which are essential, and Rousseau turned to China and learnt them there. Another is that he may have got some slight stimulus from Chinese thought; but, since there is no direct evidence in his works or letters that he was conscious of any debt to China, therefore it is to be assumed that he did all the essential work in his own mind, milling over western traditions, classical, Christian, and those arising out of the Renaissance, and from these materials created his new philosophy of man in society. My own opinion is that the truth lies between these two extremes. He was influenced deeply, more than he knew. As with so many great, original minds the source of what went into him was largely immaterial to him. Anything and everything was grist to his mill, and, when it had been ground in his unconscious mind, it came out as Rousseau and no one else. He was not concerned with Chinese thought as Chinese, in the way that Voltaire was; and in this he was more sincere, for Voltaire had an axe to grind. He used China as a stick with which to beat his enemies, clericalism and superstition. Rousseau was the far more real personality, just as he has been the far more influential teacher. To him more than to any other man, modern Europe and America owe the humanistic developments in their religion: what now some thinkers are beginning to call the great modern heresy.[1]

Leibniz and Rousseau in Later Developments of Thought

Our attention has been directed to Leibniz and Rousseau, not to Voltaire and Dr. Quesnay. The reason is clear. The latter were more conspicuous in their day and they neglected no opportunity of exciting admiration for Chinese philosophy. In this they were good propagandists; but the interest which they aroused was not a deep and lasting one. True, that by his citation of the Chinese scholars as the pattern of rationally religious men Voltaire reinforced the tendency of his day to agnosticism in religion. True, that Dr. Quesnay was the founder of the modern science of Political Economy. But the influence was deeper than along these lines, and it is in Leibniz and Rousseau that we find the evidence. Nature is superior to Reason: not that man can dispense with Reason, but its use to him is as a good servant: it makes a dangerous master. Nature as a harmony beyond the power of Law to embody, Reality as having at its core an unanalysable individuality, and this the ground of 'the contingent' in the universe as it is, the germ of human spiritual personality, these are the basic convictions in Leibniz's monadology as they are in the Confucianist philosophy of the universe. The common man with all his private-mindedness, but none the less with his sprouts of goodness and ability to actualize the general will, these are the basic convictions in Rousseau's political philosophy, and, although he carried these principles to

[1] Cp. Jacques Maritain, the learned and ardent French Catholic. M. Maritain has written what seems to me an unpardonably prejudiced study of Rousseau in his *Three Reformers*, London, 1936.

libertarian conclusions which were not visualized by Confucianist philosophers, their basic affirmations were the same.

It is these ideas which have had so great an influence in Europe and America. To give but two illustrations where a hundred of varying significance are waiting to be explored,[1] we turn to Immanuel Kant in Germany, and the political reformers and the rise of Romanticism in England. To Kant, studying in his little hide-bound university at Königsberg, there were two men who stirred his soul, in his earlier days Leibniz, in his later Rousseau. It must suffice to point to his 'categorical imperative,' that sense of duty which is man's by virtue of his nature, and his emphasis on 'the Will,' namely, that in man which in one way is so much less reliable than Reason and in another and deeper way can and does accomplish what mere logic cannot.

In England, Locke was the admired philosopher, not Leibniz, who, if he was known at all, was regarded as a weaver of fantasies. Locke, with his sensationalism and its common sense, with his essentially utilitarian mind, took his stand on the established order, the alliance of Church and State and the 'glorious liberties' which Englishmen enjoyed through the Revolution of 1688. Yes, England was a Whig paradise with money pouring in from adventures overseas, money to be spent on Chinese gardens and Chinese porcelain. But there was no room for Chinese philosophy in people's minds. Morality was utility, and that was all there was to it. And if the poor were not satisfied with life it was part of the original sin in them. But this typical eighteenth-century *haute-bourgeoisie* complacency could not last. In the eighties things began to stir. Some men began to look at life with new eyes, and this time it was under the influence of Rousseau's challenge. So the movement for political reform came into being, with

[1] In Professor Chu's work the direct and indirect influence of Chinese thought on the French Revolution thinkers is carefully worked out. Also he gives a separate chapter to the influence in Germany and carries the historical argument on to Kant, Fichte, Schelling, Hegel, and finally Schopenhauer.

men like Holcroft, Tom Paine, and Godwin, the author of *Political Justice*, as leaders. They were rationalists for the most part, believing in Laws and Rights of Nature as demonstrated by Reason, not understanding Nature as above Reason. But then came Coleridge and Wordsworth, poets of Nature—in his first enthusiasm Wordsworth a poet of revolution. There were also Blake and Shelley, each in his own way having the Rousseau philosophy of man's goodness: Blake, perhaps the greatest of all English poets after Shakespeare, since in that mystically religious mind of his he was able to blend the sphere of Nature and the sphere of Grace.

It is, of course, not claimed that the inspiring power which, for example, Kant and Wordsworth exercised in the West, is due to some magic virtue from the mystic East or the rational East, or whatever east rhapsodists like to imagine as existing. But it is claimed that in certain concrete forms, and in relation to certain highly original thinkers, notably Leibniz and Rousseau, Chinese thought entered into the main stream of European thought.

The Situation To-day

Ernst Troeltsch, the most profoundly learned of modern historians in the history of European thought, was asked in 1922, when he was an old man, to lecture to a select gathering in Berlin. He chose as his theme 'The Ideas of Natural Law and Humanity in World Politics.' The lecture was, as Professor Ernest Barker has said, written 'under the impulse of the German defeat.'[1] Troeltsch contrasted what he called the German way and the West-European way, and he does this with an immensely impressive list of distinctions. Take the following, for example:

Here we touch the core of the contrast. We begin to see on the one side, an eternal, rational, and divinely ordained system of Order, embracing both morality and law; we begin to see,

---

[1] Barker's *Natural Law and the Theory of Society, 1500-1800*, by *Otto Gierke*, with a *Lecture on the Ideas of Natural Law and Humanity by Ernst Troeltsch*. Cambridge, 1934, p. xv.

on the other, individual, living, and perpetually new incarnations of an historically creative Mind. Those who believe in an eternal and divine Law of Nature, the Equality of Man, and a sense of unity pervading mankind, and who find the essence of Humanity in these things, cannot but regard the German doctrine as a curious mixture of mysticism and brutality. Those who take an opposite view—who see in history an ever-moving stream, which throws up unique individualities as it moves, and is always shaping individual structures on the basis of a law which is always new—are bound to consider the West-European world of ideas as a world of cold rationalism and equalitarian atomism, a world of superficiality and Pharisaism.

We may well doubt whether Troeltsch, if he had lived, would have found the Nazi philosophy to his taste: but how clearly we can see some, at any rate, of the elements out of which that heady brew has been concocted. But the real point is that, as he paints the picture of German Romanticism, numberless Englishmen and Frenchmen, and certainly Americans, will feel that this expresses much of what they themselves think. They will not recognize their own tradition under the opprobrious terms of his description. And yet there is a real sense in which Troeltsch is right up to a certain point. There is a contrast between Nature and Reason, though we are never done with determining what Nature means and what Reason. And the German appears here as worshipping at the shrine of Nature and the West-European at the shrine of Reason.

The truth, surely, is that neither German nor West-European has a monopoly in either Nature or Reason, and when it comes to respect for individuality and personality the West-European is shocked at what is to him so glaringly patent, a wicked atomism in the Nazi philosophy.

To all this the cynic has his criticism to offer: both sides in this present war are laying Europe in ruins for the same principles, or rather, affectation of the same principles. His words have some truth in them. But the plain man who is never a cynic—the dog who returns to his own vomit—will have none of this, whether he be German or British. On the British side he cannot blind his eyes to certain things which he sees, and seeing he finds no option but to fight for that thing which disguises itself in so many forms, is so deceptive and yet so real, political liberty. He sees also that the Chinese people have for the last three years been doing the same for themselves and the world at large. How far this is Nature, how far Reason, and how far Religion, is the question.

The Middle Way

To the Chinese a very vivid and historically real part of their Great Tradition is the time when, as in Europe now, certain great states swallowed up the smaller, and finally stood facing each other armed to the teeth. One of these states had reorganized its life on the totalitarian principle, with a view of human nature behind it very like that which Hobbes, the Englishman, set forth in his *Leviathan*. This state beat the others in the Armageddon, and for some thirty years all North China was under Nazi rule. The Nazi leader, the First Emperor, as he called himself, gave peace to the world, but it was his kind of peace, a peace of regimentation. It was one of the great ironies of history that he commanded the Great Wall to be built and that a million men died and their bodies were shovelled into the wall, built to keep barbarism *out* of the Middle Kingdom!

The regime crashed when the First Emperor died—may we say, inevitably? The Goerings and Goebbelses and Ribbentrops at the top were, of course, not prepared to take orders from each other. After years of fighting the new regime which emerged was headed by a man who started life as a village bully. He was wise enough to see what the people wanted, not the peace of regimentation, but the peace of being left alone. The country recovered, but there was no spiritual principle set up to foster a general will. Rich men grew richer, poor men poorer. Finally, towards the end of the second century B.C. the fifth Han Emperor turned to the Confucianist scholars as Constantine turned to the

Christian bishops. Confucianism became the state religion, the position it occupied until 1912.

There were several brands of Confucianism, one sort and another growing up from the days in which Confucius himself taught (551–478 B.C.). But Confucianists themselves regarded their 'Way' as the 'Middle Way,' in contrast to the exaggerations of the Mohists, the Taoists, the Legalists (called above, the Nazis), and all the other schools of thought. This idea they owed in some measure to Confucius, but most of all to the author of the book my reader is presumably going to study, the one which I have called *The Mean-in-action*. This book survived the 'burning of the books' by the First Emperor, as did *The Great Learning*, and more or less complete versions of other earlier Confucianist works. In these books was found the spiritual principle which could make a society. In them the principles of association and the principles of government could be studied. They exalted Nature, they gave Reason its place; and 'Nature' was not a mere mechanical system of Natural Laws, but Heaven, and 'Reason' was the logic of human relationship through which human personality came into flower.

I commend, therefore, these two books to my reader. He may find them wise, or he may not; but he can hardly find them irrelevant, for to-day we have in most practical fashion to decide what we mean by Nature and what by Reason. Above all, we have to put into action the General Will under Heaven. Personally I believe Christian Europe can help to do this, but not without a new kind of Christian humility.

CHAPTER II

THE CHANGES THAT COME IN A 'GREAT TRADITION' AND
THEIR PREDICTABILITY AND UNPREDICTABILITY

A CENTURY after Rousseau's death (1778) China was still being ruled by that Manchu Court, the existence of which had proved to Rousseau that the people of that great country had a slave mentality. With all the problems which the oncoming white man forced on China, these Manchus were no help but an incubus; and yet it seemed as if nothing could dislodge them. Nevertheless, twenty years later, there were 'the Hundred Days of Reform,' due to the efforts of a group of ardent Confucianist scholars, and thirteen years later the dynasty crashed, and a republic was founded. Of the men who made this revolution two stand out above all others, Sun Yat-sen, the deracinated Christian medical doctor who had soaked his mind with western political theory as he read in the British Museum Library; and Liang Ch'i-ch'ao, who saw in western science and western democracy the fulfilment of the Chinese Great Tradition. To both these men Rousseau was a prophet, and his democratic interpretation of the 'General Will,' the saving truth about society and its government. The slogan of the revolution was *Hsin Min*,[1] the renovation of the people; and the principle of it was that only the people could renovate themselves.

That Republican China, through the force of western influence of all kinds, has been changing its traditional forms of life and of thought is a matter of common knowledge. That it has been discovering new meanings in its sacred tradition is not so well known. And it is too often believed that before the Republic came the Chinese race had been subject to a tyrannous system of hard-and-fast dogma for two thousand odd years without material change.

[1] Cp. the beginning of *The Great Learning*.

Any such idea is, of course, nonsense. However great a culture may be, if it does not renew itself, if the underlying principles of its tradition do not get thought out afresh, and new principles be not brought in to reinforce the cogency of the old, that culture will decay and die. And these changes are very often marked by change of geographical centre, introducing new racial features as well as those of climate.

We take this as a matter of course with the culture of western Europe, with its origins in Greece and Rome, the spread of their civilization to the Peninsula and Gaul, and so to Germany and Britain and Scandinavia. With the coming of a new universal religion from a Semitic country new forces began to function, not only in the old centres of culture, but also in the far-off provinces. The outcome, after the barbarian invasion when those parts of the world had settled down to their feudal regimes, was that the Graeco-Roman tradition had been changed and had become Christian. By the end of the Middle Ages there were vigorous centres of this culture, capitals of learning, as far apart as Paris, Salamanca, Prague, and Oxford. These were more significant for the future than the old centres of Athens and Rome. In a word, new peoples, adapted to northern climates, and possessing their own physical and spiritual gifts, were at work on the Great Tradition. This became doubly clear when the Renaissance movement had had time to spread. Although it involved concentration on the ancient North Mediterranean literature, in middle Europe, and, more particularly, the north and extreme west, the outcome was Protestantism. That was not so in the Mediterranean countries.

The Chinese Race and the Beginnings of their Civilization

The Chinese are not a homogeneous race, nor do they possess a homogeneous culture. Recent archaeological discoveries have been illuminating for very early times, and we now have some remarkable evidence on which to base theories of origin. Nevertheless, the one safe generalization is that the further north of the Yangtze basin the people are, the more Mongol they are, the more Tartar the strain; big-boned stalwart men and women, who live mainly on millet and, in the north-west, on the sheep which they breed. The further south of the Yangtze the people are, the more pronounced is the Malay strain. The people there live on rice, and are small and lithe, in the coastal areas given to seafaring. Climate and food are here seen as big factors in the preservation of racial distinction which otherwise, through cultural and political processes, tended to disappear. Further, there had been a big infiltration of central Asian blood-stocks into the main northern stream, and then later these mixed families, by transplantation of regional populations from north to south and from east to west, penetrated to the far south.

The cultural history of the Chinese people is even more varied. When pre-history changes to documentable history, the vigorous Chou culture is found flourishing in the lands round the Yellow River. This was the ground-stock of the later culture. But as a ground-stock it was the outcome of a grafting process between two Bronze Age cultures, the pre-historical Chou from the north-west, and the Shang-Yin; and the Shang-Yin was itself the outcome of earlier distinctive cultures in the North China area. During the Chou political era (eleventh century to 246 B.C.) something worthy of the name of a civilization emerged, and with it the Chinese people were ripe for expansion. They spread south, south-east, and south-west. Wherever they went they absorbed the indigenous tribes and inculcated their own tradition. In the end, however, the great Han dynasty (206 B.C.–A.D. 220) overreached itself. It became too unwieldly to be able to resist outside attack and civil dissension. As happened in Europe about the same time, there were four long centuries of recurrent turmoil involving large sections of the population. Capitals were set up in new centres, east and west, north and south. The north and south divisions made for the biggest cultural change, for a pure Tartar tribe held sway in the north and enhanced the influence of Buddhism in the form which it had taken on during its spread from Central Asia. Meanwhile, although the peasants stayed by the land, many of the aristocratic families, that is to say, the more conscious upholders of the indigenous Great Tradition, moved south into the Yangtze area, where life started again under different climatic conditions. Thus Confucianism, with all its strong points and all its weak, went through a process of stern testing. How stern this was became clear in the seventh century when the famous Li Shih-min, of half Chinese, half Tartar blood, united the Chinese people again under one government. The new capital, Ch'ang-an, became a home for all the religions of Asia, amongst them Nestorian Christianity.

Confucianism Unable to Hold its Own

This T'ang epoch (620–907) is one of the really great epochs in world history, politically significant like Charlemagne's regime in Europe with the revival of the Roman Empire, and amazingly potent in its cultural achievements. There was an uprush of new powers expressing themselves in religion and art, in literature and craftsmanship, in the scholar's painstaking work of exegesis done in well-stocked libraries, the poet's exquisite response to Nature, and the simple monk's finding of his real self in the common life of his Order. To confine our attention to religion, this age came to speak of 'the Three Religions.' Of these Confucianism in the main part and Taoism to a lesser degree were the Great Tradition, but Buddhism had pushed its way in, and had thrown weird contrasted lights on life and the universe. By T'ang times that fundamental intellectual simplicity and ethical austerity which the reader will find in *The Mean-in-action* and *The Great Learning*, appealed to the few rather than the many to whom life was a rich sensation whether in the cultivation of aesthetic taste or the exploration of theological paradoxes.

To the historian the whole epoch is excitingly paradoxical.

On the one hand, Confucianism, predominantly this-worldly and avowing that art had its place in the good life, was not responsible for the developments in art. As a matter of fact, the State Religion was on the defensive, with the result that it became more this-worldly than ever, concentrating on man's duty to the State. Also, with a view to making itself more popular, it began to ape Buddhist temple practices, and, as may be supposed, thereby did itself no particular good. Buddhism, on the other hand, so essentially other-worldly, was in all sorts of ways an inspiration in art; and this while the logic of its other-worldliness was driving its intellectualists to the assertion that the world was not only an illusion, but could not properly be said to exist at all. Further, in Buddhism the most striking product of the epoch was the rise of the Ch'an (Zen) sect amongst the other sects which emerged. This sect was—to use western ideology—a characteristically Chinese Protestant revolt against the dominant Catholic emphasis on rule and rite: that emphasis which claimed that purity was to be attained by ascetic penances, and by the devotional thrill which comes from the worship of sacred relics. To the Ch'an devotees the individual must become right in himself, if he is to achieve 'the Great Illumination,' and without this all the rules and rites in the revealed Scriptures must be valueless and even detrimental. That was what China could do to Buddhism. In a word, at the very time when it seemed that the old religion might go down before the greater spiritual power of the new, it was able to get in this fashion a reaffirmation of the principle that the saved man was only he who had a positively integrated ethical personality.

This was a new China which had come into existence, more subtle in its thinking, more refined in its taste, many of its people concerned with a kind of salvation which the old China of classical days had not visualized. The attraction of the contemplative life, for women as well as for men, was so great that officials saw, with dismay, the business of the State impeded by the withdrawal of so many from the active population. In this society the Confucianist Scriptures were still studied, among them *The Mean-in-action* and *The Great Learning*; but we have no evidence that they really fed men's minds and souls except in the case of two men to whom we shall come presently. The lively, inquiring minds of the day found a more satisfying diet elsewhere. It was, therefore, unpredictable what was going to happen, what this new China actually was going to be. One thing only is clear, that although defence reasons made it necessary for the capital to be in the northwest, the wealth and culture of the country was tending more and more to go south.

Two Unpredictable Developments in Western History

We need to pause a moment and look to more familiar fields for cases of an old-established spiritual culture which is assailed by new and, at any rate, more exciting ideas from abroad, assailed also by the fact that the social conditions are different from what they were long ago in a past which seems by contrast simple and less civilized. The most apposite one seems to be the crisis in Europe in the thirteenth century. Arab culture, to the Church's leaders an insidious poison, was capturing the best minds, whilst the whirlwind advance of the Mongol hordes made people wonder whether Christian culture would survive at all. There arose the great Scholastic system, fathered by that extraordinary combination of philosopher and theologian, St. Thomas Aquinas, who, in his quiet, laborious fashion simply broke away from the Aristotelian premises. Europe rallied from its doubts. Men gained a new confidence in their Great Tradition. They felt they could face the world. And yet what a weight of speculative intellectualization this new philosophy laid on the Christian mind.

We may turn also to the Jews at the end of the first century B.C. when Hellenism, like a tide, came seeping into their minds and changing their whole outlook on life. We know what the Pharisees and Zealots tried to do, and what, on the other hand, Philo and his friends in Alexandria thought was the way to save Judaism alive. We know also how a movement started by a young carpenter upset all calculations of trends and tendencies and gave to the world a new and potent religion. These are major events in history, and, after they have happened, they can be rationalized this way and that. But the question is whether they can be predicted in their uniqueness before they happen.

Two T'ang Thinkers and 'The Great Learning' and 'The Mean-in-action'

The strength of the Buddhist appeal lay in its subtle understanding of the individual, and the promise it gave of a glorious release from the chains of desire. As we look back we can see that the problem for the T'ang Confucianists, if they were to recapture men's faith in the Great Tradition, was to discover an equally convincing promise for the individual without the Buddhist weaknesses of over-introspection and over-subtlety of thought. Actually the old guard stressed duty to the State and called on the emperors to put down the foreign cult with a strong hand. Also, as a sop to the populace and its obvious passion for worshipping somebody, they made Confucius a god, calling him *Hsuan Fu* (Great Father, or, it may be, Universal Father). In all this they constantly invoked the authority of the State, but exercised no new self-authenticating authority over men's minds.

The greatest in the ranks of this old guard was Han Yü, China's Cato. He was not only a statesman, calling for the shirkers, the monks and nuns, to be driven back to the sacred obligations of daily life, but also an apologist with a keen mind and a command of living expression. In addition to this, he went looking for new light on the function of desire in the economy of man's life: desire which his opponents claimed to have plumbed to its very depths. In the pursuit of his end he turned to *The Great Learning*. His disciple, Li Ao, went a step further. He pored over

The Mean-in-action and found there a new meaning to the reality in man's personality and the reality in heaven and earth; for that was the point at issue between the Buddhists and the Confucianists. What he discovered was a mystical significance to the reality (*ch'eng*)[1] there set forth, a reality not divorced from the ethical, but having wider implications. To him not only man's desires, but also his powers of thinking, were an obstacle to this search for reality; for thinking leads to action, and action destroys the inward calm in which alone the light of reality can shine forth. Li Ao here betrays the influence of Buddhist and, more particularly, Taoist ways of thinking. The terms he used were, many of them, those to which the ancient Taoist mystics had attached so deep a meaning. He was, indeed, a contemplative, looking at life from the contemplative's point of view.

The Sung Epoch

The T'ang regime collapsed at the end of the ninth century. There was little peace in China for the next sixty years. What there was was in the south and extreme west where the natural wealth in the soil made better social conditions more possible. The spirit of the T'ang culture survived there in greater force; and when Chao Kuang-yin, the military leader who saw beyond military dominance, appealed to the southerners as Chinese to join with him in making a Chinese unity and peace, the response was wholehearted. Thus the famous pacific Sung dynasty came into existence. But there was no telling whether the dominant spiritual force in this new China was to be Confucianism or Buddhism, for, although Manichaeism and Nestorian Christianity had vanished in the fires of the T'ang persecutions, Buddhism had not. It was as strong as ever.

The striking characteristic of this epoch is that, although it inherited the treasures of the T'ang literature and art and appreciated them, yet it went its own way, developing its own excellences in these fields and, most significant of all,

Cp. *Mean-in-action*, c. 21 et seq.

evolving new powers of philosophizing. In the old days it was Taoism which attracted the more subtle metaphysical minds, whilst there were other schools which were concerned with the problems of speculative knowledge. The movement which started with Confucius gave the weight of its attention mainly to the ethical and its corollary the socio-political. The Confucianists had their cosmological theories, but these were quite crude systems; and, although stress was laid upon knowledge, the main content of knowledge was either the sacred tradition handed down from the past or the practical wisdom which enabled a man to serve the needs of his age. Classical Confucianism may be said to have produced only one first-class metaphysician, the author of *The Mean-in-action*. The Sung epoch, however, has the proud distinction of producing quite a number of good metaphysicians and men who attacked the problems of knowledge with real ardour; and the significant thing is that they all regarded themselves as good Confucianists.

Throughout the eleventh and twelfth centuries there was a succession of these men who set themselves to discover the truth about the universe. They were immensely individual in their lines of thought: as individual as the T'ang poets had been in their way, or as the early Greek scientists had been, or the outstanding figures of the Protestant Reformation in western Europe. Also, they were men of learning, familiar with the Taoist and Buddhist ideologies as well as with that of traditional Confucianism. The result was new categories of thought, new principles on which men could base their *a priori* assumptions. How rich was the variety of their speculations we hardly know to-day, for later thinkers became so absorbed in the dogmas of what became the Great Orthodoxy and in the tenets of its opponent, the Liu-Wang School, that they did not do justice to the less famous fruits of Sung thought. Some of them have survived, tucked away in old compendia, handed down by bookworms to whom a book is precious just because it is old. But the work of appraisal is waiting for the modern historian-philosopher.

Confucianism thus came to hold its own again, indeed, to strengthen its hold on Chinese minds. Buddhism never regained its earlier power. Before we consider this new kind of Confucianism which swung Chinese thought away from excessive transcendentalism to another form of this-worldliness, we must note one factor in the Sung situation; for it may account quite largely for the unprecedented attention which came to be given to *The Great Learning* and *The Mean-in-action*. This factor was the rapid development of printing. According to the evidence from the Tung Huan caves, the Buddhists were the first to realize the value of duplicating for evangelizing purposes. In Sung times, therefore, it was just as likely, at least, that Buddhists should have made the most profitable use of it. Apparently they did not, and the reason may be advanced that their intelligent readers were mainly monks, whilst Confucianists were more often in the world. Thus with their intelligence sharpened by contact with affairs, the scholars were able to reap the full benefit of being, for the first time, able to study the whole body of their sacred literature. In earlier times it was, of course, much more difficult to get books, with the result that the man who was proficient in one section of the Scriptures was regarded as worthy of the status of a scholar; if he was proficient in two sections he was a very good scholar.

The significance of this for the study of *The Great Learning* and *The Mean-in-action* lies in the fact that these two works had been rescued after the First Emperor's time by the upholders of the traditional ritual, and they had finally been embodied in a compendium on ritual. They were, in consequence, the subject of study to men who found their satisfaction in ritual; not the kind of men to be distinguished for philosophic or prophetic vision. This state of affairs would continue so long as the manuscripts of the Scriptures could not be duplicated on a large scale. Thus, the expounding of *The Great Learning* and *The Mean-in-action* was done by antiquarian minds. When, however, all parts of the Scriptures became accessible to scholars of all kinds, then something might be expected to happen. And this was the more likely because it was now possible to organize private colleges (*shu yuan*) with good libraries. The Sung epoch saw the beginning of this practice, one destined to exercise a great influence in later ages.

The Emergence of the Ch'eng-Chu School

The Great Orthodoxy referred to above is the Neo-Confucianism of the Ch'eng-Chu School. To modern ears anything orthodox sounds particularly dull; but every orthodox system once had its thrilling beginning when some enterprising thinker first conceived some new theory, worked it out, and then found that it was good food for hungry minds. This is what happened in the case of Chu Hsi (1129-1200), the man who, for over half a millennium, right down to the beginning of the twentieth century, was generally regarded as the first man to understand the truth in the teachings of Confucius and his disciples. It took Chu Hsi long years to evolve his system of thought, and, as he evolved it, he had to fight hard for it against its critics. To his disciples it was immensely stimulating. It seemed to them to have 'bones and sinews.'

The upshot of Chu Hsi's quest for truth was that he found his main inspiration in *The Great Learning* and *The Mean-in-action*. But his mind had a long way to go before it arrived at this point. After his formal education his attention was attracted to much more varied fields of learning. He studied the Taoist Fathers and the Buddhist Scriptures. These left him with a feeling of profound dissatisfaction. The Buddhist metaphysicians might be extremely subtle and open up all sorts of heights and depths; but to the young Chu Hsi, living in an age which was systematizing history, it was plainly untrue to say that this world from the beginning was nothing but illusion. So with his powers of discriminate thinking considerably enhanced Chu Hsi left these more recondite fields and went back to the Confucianist books.

He then discovered the writings of the two brothers, Ch'eng Ming-tao and Ch'eng Yi-ch'uan (1032–1108). These proved immensely illuminating, particularly Yi-ch'uan's part of them, for he had a gift of keen analysis. He was awake to the problems which arise over the distinction between the material and the non-material, and the mysterious border-line between the two. Yi-ch'uan was also something of a higher critic. Thus from *The Great Learning* and *The Mean-in-action* he got new vistas of truth, but the text, as he read them, puzzled him. *The Great Learning*, in particular, did not make the systematic sense that he felt he had reason to expect. He propounded the theory, therefore, that in the early days of the book's existence the text had got into disorder and had remained so ever since. Acting on this theory, Yi-ch'uan set to work and rearranged the whole of the middle of the book, so that he did get sense. Only, he then discovered that at one very important point in the argument (according to his arrangement) there was a big hole. What the argument required to be discussed was not discussed. He assumed, in consequence, that part of the original text had been lost.

To Chu Hsi, with his passion for getting things clear and coherent, all this was meat and drink. With the new order of *The Great Learning* to guide him he found the great affirmations at the beginning of the book thrown into sharp relief. He became convinced that the tradition which made Confucius the author of these was right. He took them, sentence by sentence, word by word, and applied them in every field of thought and action, not resting till the *pen* and the *mo* (the trunk and the branches) were clear to him. In this task he found *The Mean-in-action* equally illuminating. Consequently, when he had made his synthesis, he laid it down that the essence of the Confucianist tradition was contained in these two works along with the record of Confucius's own sayings in the *Analects* and the record of Mencius's teachings in the book under his name. It is, then, from Chu Hsi's time, and not before, that these works have been known as *The Four Books*, and have been made the centre of education in right thinking and right living.

The Limitations of Chu Hsi's Synthesis

In Chapter I it was stated: '"Nature" in classical Confucianism, and even in Neo-Confucianism, is not a wholly mechanical chain of cause and effect, but something living in the fullest sense, characterized by what Leibniz called "the contingent" as well as "the necessary": "the contingent," that range of possibilities, as distinct from actualities on the one hand and impossibilities on the other, which goes along with the reality of the individual and the personal.' Why that 'even in Neo-Confucianism'? Because Chu Hsi made a revolution in the Confucianism which he thought he was interpreting in terms of its original meaning. He changed the emphasis in the Great Tradition from fidelity to Nature to fidelity to Reason, from finding the truth mainly by right living to finding the truth primarily by right thinking. In his own way he made the same inference about existence that Descartes did, 'I think, therefore I am': the affirmation which gave such a list to European thought on the side of intellectualization, of the abstraction of thought from life.

The way in which Chu Hsi made this new emphasis can be seen in his treatment of the 'investigation of things' (*ko wu*),[1] the first of the eight conditions which are set forth at the beginning of *The Great Learning* as requisite, if man is to attain peace on earth. As one of the men who influenced Chu Hsi had said, 'The mind grinds on matter, and matter grinds on the mind.' He plainly set his mind to grind on things, breaking away from the profitless round of passional introspection and the technique of levitating oneself into reality by mystical mind-emptying. By this discipline, he felt, the mind could be objectified; and there is

---

[1] In the translation *ko wu* is rendered by 'appreciation of things,' which seems to me nearer to the original meaning. It was Chu Hsi who made *ko* mean investigation.

good evidence to show that he had keen observational powers, and to some extent used them on natural phenomena. It would appear, therefore, that Chu Hsi was on the verge of opening the door which Francis Bacon opened. In fact, however, he was more like St. Thomas Aquinas, an ardent student of books; that is to say, of what other men had to say about things rather than of things themselves.

As a modern scientist might say, he was a philosopher, preferring argument to observation and experiment. The criticism would be warranted. And yet it must have been through observation, for the most part, that he came to see how everything is more than the mere sum of its parts. It has its structure as a whole, the co-ordinating principle to it, by virtue of which it is that individual thing. This principle Chu Hsi called the *li* of that thing; and, since every other thing also had its *li*, the universe came to him to be a united system of *li* (plural). Thus, the universe itself, as a whole, has its *li*, its co-ordinating principle. Not only so. Those things which are sufficiently alike to make a class of things, have also a *li* as a class. Thus, *li* is the basis of comparison.

There is no doubt that Chu Hsi had a forensic mind. He loved argument, and, the more he argued, the more he lost sight of the fact that, when he thought he was investigating things as they are, he was actually investigating their co-ordinating principles as he thought them to be. That, of course, makes a lot of difference when a man is trying to think in terms of the reality of the universe. Wang Yang-ming, Chu Hsi's great Ming era opponent, brought this out in his famous gibe:

I pointed to some bamboos in front of a pavilion and asked my friend to investigate them. Day and night he went into the investigation of their *li*, applying his whole mind to it for the space of three days. Finally, he was exhausted and fell ill. At first I said that it was because his powers were not equal to the task, so I undertook to go on with the investigating myself. Day and night I tried to understand the *li* of the bamboos; but in vain. Eventually, after seven days, I also fell ill through the sheer strain of thinking. The result was that my friend and I sighed to each other and said: 'Since we have not the powers to carry out an investigation of things, therefore we cannot be sages or men of great virtue!'

From this angle it is clear how Chu Hsi tended away from fidelity to Nature to fidelity to Reason; for the more he was involved in elucidating the nature of this *li* and the other, particularly when dealing with classes of things, the more his mind was acting under the influence of his speculative reason. Hence the accusation that he substituted *li* for the classical Confucianist's *T'ien* (Heaven) is essentially true. A similar accusation may be brought against the ethical part of his synthesis. Whereas the classical Confucianists thought primarily in terms of given natural relationships between man and man, Chu Hsi stressed virtues, that is to say, ideals of conduct, *jen* (benevolence), *yi* (fair dealing), *chung* (reverence), *chih* (understanding), and *hsin* (good faith). These are essentially abstractions of the mind, not like given relationships. And the same applies to his use of the old concept of *chung-yung*, the central idea of *The Mean-in-action*. As we shall see, it was not defined by the original author as a golden mean between two extremes of action. But to Chu Hsi it meant precisely that, and he made it as such a controlling rule in human conduct, a law encouraging certain types of action, notably the law-abiding. Whilst, therefore, we may acclaim his synthesis as a momentous event in the history of Chinese thought, putting *The Gerat Tradition* on a higher level of logical coherence, on the other hand, we have to mark its susceptibility to being made into hard and fast dogma as also into the tool of political privilege.

Reality as Substance or as Relation

As we saw in Chapter I, there is a close affinity between Chu Hsi's philosophy of *li* and Leibniz's philosophy of the monad. Interesting as that is, there is something even more interesting in connection with these two thinkers. They bring out the main distinction between a western and a Chinese tradition in pure philosophy.[1] The western has tended to see reality as substance, the Chinese to see it as relationship. Behind the metaphysical idea of 'substance' lies the logical idea of 'identity'; and western philosophers laid down as a basic principle of thought that a thing cannot both be and not be at the same time. Chinese philosophers, on the other hand, laid down that a thing is always either becoming or de-becoming, if the term may be allowed. It is all the time on the way to being something else. Thus the idea of 'identity' is blurred. This contrast in the two traditions may be illustrated by saying that the one tended to think of the material universe in terms of its chemistry, the other in terms of its physics, the characteristic feature of which is the *Yang* and the *Yin*, constructive and destructive forces for ever at work in everything.

Now how Chu Hsi fitted his system of *li* in with this *yang* and *yin* process is beyond the scope of an introduction, even one which goes so far afield as this one. But what does concern us is that by his *li* he opened the door to the reality of 'substance,' whilst Leibniz with his monads opened the door to the reality of 'relationship.' Thus the two traditions show signs of being able to meet. Alongside of this we can place the fact that in the borderline between chemistry and physics the modern study of 'matter' has, to all appearances, cut the ground away from the old logic built on the identity of the atom. The atom is now seen to consist of a nucleus and a number of electrons, mysterious centres of energy which are in relation—one might even say a *yang* and *yin* relation—to each other and never keep still. In fact, all that can be said about them is that they are neither here nor there at any given moment of time, but that they are in relation. In these circumstances the question is what metaphysics will be in the future.

---

[1] This distinction has been explored by Chang Tun-sung, a contemporary philosopher. A statement of his views is given in English in an article in the *Yenching Journal of Social Studies*, vol. i.

Predictable Reason and Unpredictable Reason

The plain man is not concerned with the niceties of distinction which philosophers make. On the other hand, he is vastly concerned with finding some sort of reality in life. The main cause of our modern distress is the carking suspicion that not only has the bottom dropped out of what our fathers took to be reality, but also there is no such thing as reality at all. The result is, frequently, complete cynicism, in itself a negation of living and next door to suicide, or, more often, the taking of refuge in some patently jerry-built reality which will keep a man going for the time being. It is thus that the latest product of revolutionary logic has its attraction, just as at the time when *The Great Learning* was written the Legalist theory of man's nature attracted the people who had lost confidence in life. The theory was so logically convincing, particularly as its primary affirmation was that the present state of affairs is intolerable and, therefore, the precise opposite must be brought into being. Reason does not hesitate to predict. It is only Nature, Nature which asserts itself so unpredictably in history, that bids us look carefully before we commit ourselves too confidently to the logic of our immediate circumstances.

That part of China's cultural history which we have been examining appears to illustrate this with exceptional clarity. Confucius and his disciples did something radical to the old tribal religion. Whilst retaining most of the old ritual, they filled it with a new and higher ethical content, and gave a universal meaning to the old myths and legends. The heroes of antiquity became sage-kings. Thus, as M. Henri Bergson[1] would put it, Chinese religion became mixed, part static, part dynamic, in some respects fitted to conserve the unity of society, in other respects placing the individual in relation to his fellow man on the basis of a common humanity under Heaven. This was the Confucianism which

[1] Cp. *Les Deux Sources de la moralité et de la religion.* Paris, 1932. English translation by Andra and Bereton, London, 1935. One of the most significant books of this generation.

the Han Emperor, Han Wu Ti, established and endowed in the society of his empire. The danger, however, of an established religion is that it may come unconsciously to submerge the man in the subject. To the extent to which it does this it lapses back into the condition of being a static religion of a closed society. The Confucianism of T'ang times, when compared with Buddhism and its universalism, is seen at once to have gone that way; and it is equally plain that this is why its influence declined. Then, however, came the Sung renaissance. The dynamic element was reinforced, man was taught to see himself again as man, but this time with the dangerous implication that all-embracive Heaven (Nature) was equivalent to Reason.

We must again emphasize that this was a new China with all the rich variety of aesthetic and intellectual consciousness which the T'ang and Sung epochs had brought its people. With this there had come to be a proud consciousness of cultural unity so that in times of confusion there was no move to split China into separate States. She remained one in spite of the disruptive effects of two barbarian invasions, the Mongol and the Manchu. Whether the decisive factor here was the elevation of the Ch'eng-Chu philosophy into a high tyranny of State-supported dogma is an open question. It may well be that what the *Torah* of the scribes did for the Jews in Roman times, the *Li Hsüeh* of the scholars did for China in more modern times: for this would be the hard core to the culture, maintaining under new conditions the sense of racial identity. If that be so, it was at a heavy cost, as emerged to view when the Chinese had to face the invasion of the West. The dynamic element in their religion had become overlaid by the static element. The old self-regarding pyschology of the tribe reasserted itself, the pyschology which marshals all its forces to resist outside interference of any kind. The heavy, self-complacent arrogance with which the majority of the scholars met the challenge of western learning was a denial of the best in their Great Tradition.

There would seem to be a peculiarly severe nemesis

attached to the narrowing of life to fit the Procrustean bed of a long-established set of dogmas. I am tempted to use the mysterious saying in the New Testament about 'the sin against the Holy Ghost' which 'shall not be forgiven.' The sin is the self-satisfied conviction that all truth has been revealed to my society, my Church, to me. And this brings us to the philosopher's problem which we have been examining in this chapter: Is the reality of the universe one of substance, or one of relation, or what? Here is a test of whether a society is in the main a closed society or an open one. The typical closed society obviously devotes its energies of mind and soul to preserving itself as an identity. It is sharply conscious of the distinction, either I exist or I do not exist, in which latter case I am nothing. Further, I must exist as I am or I do not exist at all. Further, if my effort to maintain existence is successful, then it follows that there must be substance reality in my Great Tradition.

Reason in so arguing is true to its trade, for its function, as the scientists keep on insisting, is to deal with the ponderable and the definable. This side of man's nature has an ineradicable tendency to limit thought and action to the beaten track, only moving out into Nature's unknown when it feels sure of its ground. Its aim is, above all, to achieve lasting security: an aim approved by Nature up to a certain point; for without certain reliable sequences of day and night, without action producing pleasure and pain as quickly reminding semaphores, man cannot achieve his habitual round, and without that he dies. But, if Reason serves us well up to this point, it does not follow that all life can be interpreted in terms of security. In the last resort, for every man that means my security, the necessary condition of my survival. Nature will not have this; and nowhere is this more clear than in a large society living on the level of a highly developed civilization. There the overweening use of Reason, buttressing the intricate machinery of organization by ever more intricate machinery, seeks to stabilize by ingenuity of device the life of that society along the familiar line of its own cultural and material progress.

Nature is the God of unceasing change as well as of temporary identity. By this we know that the reality in the universe cannot be adequately expressed in terms of substance alone. It must also be expressed in terms of relation, the relations between one changing being and other changing beings. Here there emerges to view the undeviating justice of Nature; and Justice, it will be remembered, was the connecting link which the two best philosophical minds in Greece sought to establish between man and the order of Nature. Nature in its justice is no respecter of persons, has no preference for any shadowy likeness of substance in this person or that, in this culture or that. But Nature sustains and glorifies the living relation between one person and another, one society and another, one culture and another. For in relation every being is stirred to stand outside itself, and in so far as it does this and is open to the Great Other, to that extent it lives the life of Nature. Because it gives, it is able to receive; and because it receives, it is able to give more.

Great is Reason; but Nature is greater, creating with its justice what we cannot predict. And there has been no epoch in history which can compare with that of modern western Europe and America for the triumphs of reason which have been won. Our white race has increased and multiplied and gone a long way to possess the earth. It exploited Nature to such a degree that Nature itself seemed the guardian of the cultural identity. Its high priests even thought that this exploitation was a service to the Most High God. And now the outcome is war between the more successful of the white peoples, a highly rational war which the pundits on both sides were able to predict, a war carried out with highly rational weapons, the effect of which the least intelligent can predict. Religion seems unable to intervene. But Nature—or should we say, God—does not cease from intervening, for, as the author of *The Mean-in-action* came to see, the hidden core of reality in the universe cannot be intermittent in its functioning.

CHAPTER III

THE SOCIETY WHICH PRODUCED 'THE MEAN-IN-ACTION' AND
'THE GREAT LEARNING'

BEFORE coming to the actual history of *The Mean-in-action* and *The Great Learning* it is necessary to consider the legends and myths which were current in that epoch. As in every culture they are important, partly because they may contain valuable information on the prehistory of the race, partly because they show what intelligent men of the classical era thought about the dim far-back age before them. Thus, whilst they may contain very little reliable historical material in one way, they certainly contain a very great deal in another way.

In the unindustrialized parts of Scotland and Ireland it is still possible to find men and women who implicitly believe in the old stories. In the Middle Ages nearly everybody believed them. For instance, there were Welsh princely families which, in all seriousness, traced their genealogies back to somebody in the Old Testament and so right back to Adam. The interesting thing is that such a Bible-supported tree must be a later Christian version of an earlier pre-Christian one. Thus the later version of a legend may go further back in time than its original version.

The Time Sweep in Chinese Legendary History

The accepted stories about high antiquity in China have a very impressive time-sweep to them. In terms of our western chronology—and the reader should remind himself from time to time that the Chinese have their own chronology, one of dynastic eras and epochs—the start was about 3000 B.C. Earlier than that there was a Lao Pan, an Adam kind of figure, but scholars were inclined to think that he was too far back to be a really historical person. Pao Hsi and Shen Nung, however, who taught their ancestors to use fire and to till the soil, they were the beginnings of real history and could be dated, if only approximately. There was a chronological map in people's minds, and all down the centuries teachers and professional storytellers made literates and illiterates alike familiar with such summarized expressions as 'the era of the Five Emperors' and 'the era of the Three Kings.'

The curious thing is that even after there was a canon of sacred scripture there was not a uniform account as to who these Five Emperors were. Earlier and later scriptures themselves did not agree, and there were references in non-canonical works which gave further variations. Thus earlier versions of stories peep out at us from behind the detail of later versions. In spite of these discrepancies confidence in this solid background of immense antiquity was in no way sapped. The Chinese saw themselves as a great people carrying on the traditions of a great civilization which had as its founders sage-emperors of illimitable virtue, men who had been directly inspired by Heaven, or the Supreme Ruler (*Shang Ti*), to lead the forefathers of the race into the highway of the good life. These legendary, perhaps wholly mythical, figures were, of course, as real to the Chinese as Moses and King Arthur to our forefathers.

Modern Criticism of Ancient Legends

By the eighteenth century there were critical-minded scholars who were dubious about the authenticity of the earliest sage-emperors. They took the *Document Scripture* (*Classic of History*) as their guide, and since that started with Yao (2336 B.C.) and in the *Analects* of Confucius there was mention of him and his successor, Shun, reliable history was reckoned as probably not going further back than that date. One or two daring critics even went further than that and stated grounds for questioning the historicity of Yao and Shun. Thus a definitely higher critical movement came into existence, one destined to survive and gather vitality and acumen.

The spirit of the Manchu regime was hostile to such a movement; K'ang Hsi and Ch'ien Lung made heresy the crime of sedition. Nevertheless they endowed scholarship, and within certain limits the standards of scholarship improved enormously. The tools were made which critics need. When, therefore, the dynasty fell (1911) and the establishment of the Republic brought freedom of thought, the younger scholars got to work and, amongst other things, proceeded to evaluate afresh the lore of the sage-kings. The result is that the earliest kings now appear as early Yin and early Chou mythical figures, adapted by later ages with a gift for adding legendary detail. Some eighteenth-century suggestions have been followed up, and it is clear now that the later a book is, the further its time sweep goes back, and the more detail it has to offer about the very earliest times. The distinction also is now recognized between the patron saints of different late Chou schools of thought. Thus, to put it more cynically than is perhaps warranted, the Confucianists proved the rightness of their views by claiming the authority of Yao and Shun for them. The Mohists made the great Yü the prototype of their way of serving mankind. The Taoists, coming later, went back further than the other two schools, and found in the Yellow Emperor the first exponent of Taoist principles.

This kind of interpretation is, of course, scandalous in the eyes of some old-fashioned scholars, and it may be iconoclastic in temper. But, speaking generally, the critical results are giving new China a truer appreciation of the ancient spirit of the race. To the western student, trying to see China as she really was, the stories, therefore, are not history in the simple sense. And, as he reads of the sage-kings, for instance, in *The Mean-in-action* and *The Great Learning*, he has to appreciate, not only the authors' instinctive love of the past, but also the bona-fide spirit in which they reconstructed antiquity. It stood to reason for these men of the new mind which was busy creating the China of the ages, that these heroes had had something to teach on the good life for man.

The Chou Regime and the Age in which Confucius lived

Since our two books were written by men who regarded themselves as followers of Confucius's Way, it is necessary for us to be able to place him and the society in which he lived. His dates, 551–479 B.C., are reliable to within a year or two. He was born towards the end of what is known as the Spring and Autumn period; and that was part of the Eastern Chou epoch which lasted from 770 to 256 B.C. The first half of the Chou era as a whole began in the twelfth century or thereabouts. Having invaded the Yellow River basin from the north-west and having smashed the power of the Yin chief, the Chou clans proceeded to dig themselves in over the whole area. This, it appears, took time, and its successful accomplishment with the building up of a stable regime was largely due to the statesmanship of Duke Chou, the younger brother of the conqueror. He became the tutelary hero of the fief of Lu, Confucius's native land, so that we may assume that the people there knew something about him. With his help the Chou order was set up on a definitely feudal basis, with each holder of Yin lands and ruler of Yin serfs fitting into his defined position in the feudal hierarchy. The fiefs were small in contrast with the royal demesne, and a lord knew that, if he did not discharge his due service to his chief overlord, he would be subject to attack by such of his neighbours as the king might call on to enforce his authority and, incidentally, to make a bit for themselves. This was the disciplinary side to the royal control. There was a constructive side, a regularly recurrent series of meetings for martial exercises and, above all, a special cult of King Wen, the father of King Wu and Duke Chou. To him were attributed all the mighty virtues which had put Heaven on the side of the Chou clans and brought them to power and possession. Some of the sacrificial odes to him have survived, and a study of them gives the impression that a new standard of moral earnestness was introduced into this worship. The scions of the royal house were reminded that Heaven's blessings depended on their following King Wen's great example.

Things went well for one to two hundred years. The practice of agriculture was improved and extended, as well it might be with the conquered Yin people there to do the work. China came definitely into her Iron Age. Wealth began to accumulate, and with it came the pomps and vices which accompany a successful feudal system. Then a devastating inroad by barbarian tribes was followed by a rising of the serfs in the royal demesne. Weakened by these blows King P'ing took the fateful decision to move the capital east, in the hope of becoming stronger through the support of the more powerful feudatories. The precise opposite happened. Through the Spring and Autumn period one baron after another was able to set himself up as protector to the throne, in other words to aggrandize himself at the expense of his weaker neighbours; and this in the name of the king. For a long time the process of larger fiefs eating up the smaller had been going on, and by the time the young Confucius began looking at his world the great lords were well on the way to become rulers of independent states. A certain prestige hung about the Chou court. At least, we have to assume so, for it continued for nearly three hundred years more; but the vital energies in the body politic were not in the head but entirely in the limbs.

Thus the *kuo* (countries) of which we shall read in our two books were much larger than the original fiefs and consisted in part of territory won by the sword. Each of the great lords was afraid of the others, and the main part of his working year was spent in seeing to it that his food supplies and fighting men were adequate, and in arranging that he should have friends if he was attacked or wanted to attack somebody else. Enough of the spirit and form of Duke Chou's original system survived for meetings of groups of lords to take place, for marriage alliances to be made, and solemn treaties to be drawn up. An elaborate ritual characterized these proceedings, and by this ritual we discern the existence of a code of chivalry. But the pressure of fear was very strong in these uncertain times when an old family might be wiped out. It was impossible, therefore, to tell whether a lord's sense of honour or sense of expediency would direct his actions. The old religious sanctions plainly were decaying. In the dingdong struggle of power politics the temptation arose for a man to try both ways, to put up the façade of being a man of honour, and at the same time to do that amount of cheating which circumstances seemed to compel. If he was successful, he could glorify his ancestors by rebuilding their temple and having the sacrifices to them done with enhanced solemnity. He could also pride himself on having brought prosperity to his country. What more could Heaven and his ancestors expect from him in a world such as the one he lived in?

That was the state of affairs as between one *kuo* and another. Within the boundaries of the *kuo* equally radical changes were taking place in Confucius's time. In the original instance—so the evidence seems to show—no fief was larger than fifty miles across, and the smaller ones were not more than ten miles. Under such circumstances the life of a feudal community was a simple affair. Everything depended on the seasons, peace, and the good faith of the lord. There was a personal relationship between him and his serfs, and the main lines of this were laid down by old-established customs: on the one side, so much labour on the lord's fields, so much fuel and other products for him from the open country round: and, on the other side, protection from wild beasts and raiders, free grain when the crops failed. It must have paid not to risk peasant fury by any gross contravention of custom. Moreover, in some fiefs, at least, it seems to have been the rule for the serfs to attend the sacrifices in the lord's ancestral temple, and afterwards get a festive meal of some sort. All this points to a real sense of community.

With the coming of the larger *kuo* the good elements in the situation tended to disappear. The duke in his capital had his state to keep up, his expert craftsmen to feed, his captains to reward, his presents to give to his allies. Administration would be less and less carried on in the old customary fashion. A whole set of officials was required, tax collectors, police officers, recorders of events, and, in some cases, permanent garrisons at strategic points on the borders. Trade developed, not only within the bounds of one *kuo* but between one *kuo* and the others. There were high roads to be kept in repair and markets to be administered, with market dues and customs barriers and officers in charge of them.

Another complication was the rise of forces in the State (*kuo*) which could dispute the authority of the duke himself, and even depose him and wipe him and his family out of existence. When this occurred, it was highly shocking to the neighbouring great lords; but they learned to put up with the usurpers, if they were not strong enough to bring retribution on them and parcel out the country among themselves. In Lu State in Confucius's time there were three clans known as the 'Three Han,' descendants through a concubine of a Duke Han of a century back. They constantly quarrelled with each other, but they constantly combined against their lawful head, the duke. They expected to have the chief administrative posts, and for a time they were strong enough to divide up among themselves the state militia levies and the funds ear-marked for financing them. Matters reached such a pass that the reigning duke, a pusillanimous fellow it must be confessed, joined in a plot to assassinate the Three Han's leader, Chi Tzu. The plot failed, and the next thing was that the duke and his friends were fleeing for their lives to the neighbouring Ch'i State. There was a great hullabaloo over this among the lords; but the duke never regained his position. Chi Tzu would only swear allegiance to his son. Later, when the son was duke, there was a concerted movement in which Confucius joined to destroy the strongholds of the Three Han. It should be noted that although Chi Tzu had the most violent bullying temper, we have information about other leaders of these clans which shows that they were reasonable men. One or two of them had a great respect for Confucius.

Confucius the Saint and Confucius the Man

Founders of religions seem to suffer to a peculiar degree the fate of being rationalized by later generations of their disciples. Thus the earlier accounts of a saint contain the more intimately human and realistic detail, the later make a halo for him, and, often enough, the saint has to fit the halo rather than the reverse. Confucius has not suffered so much as some, but he suffered badly enough; as we have seen, in the seventh century they tried to make him a completely divine figure. Before that, one emperor after another gave him by solemn rescript some special rite, some semi-divine, semi-political title: in some cases, it may be suspected, with the aim of enhancing the prestige of the throne as well as the authority of the sage. The first attempt at a methodical life of him, written towards the end of the second century B.C., is a curious combination of plain, straightforward chronicling and of hagiological details. The author, Ssu-ma Ch'ien, was a genius of a historian, but it is clear that by his time the figure of Confucius the man was inextricably blended with the figure of Confucius the sage.

In dealing with pre-Confucian days the historian is hampered by the extreme paucity of evidence. In dealing with the life of Confucius the situation is exactly the reverse. There are a dozen books and more which have to be consulted, and they differ considerably in the man whom they portray. The trouble is that hardly any of these accounts can be dated with any certainty within, say, a hundred years. We cannot be at all sure that the librarians of the imperial library in the first century B.C. did not have difficulties with the texts, and so, for one reason or another, introduce extraneous material. Thus there are a number of very intricate problems still waiting to be solved about Confucius the man.

One of these problems is in connection with Confucius's standing in society as a Ju. There can be no question but that he was a member of this class, in spite of what appears in Han literature. By then men were concerned to discover that the sage was of noble lineage; and, it is hardly necessary to add, they proved this to their satisfaction. To the modern historian this is very dubious, and he goes back with renewed zeal to the question of who and what the Ju were in eastern Chou society. We may take it that they were the initiates in all the numerous departments of life. Later, in the Spring and Autumn period, they came to take on all sorts of administrative duties; but in the first instance they were religious functionaries, experts in the customary ritual, and, as such, cultivated a religious prestige with their voluminous cassocks and prodigious head-dresses. Also a good case can be made out for their having been the descendants of the original Yin Ju, of men who, when the Chou clans conquered their country, carried on in the service of their conquerors. If this be so, then it helps to account for the fact that in the Spring and Autumn society we find them as a distinct class, to be distinguished from the plebeians on the one hand and the patricians on the other.

K'ung Chung-ni (Confucius) was of Ju stock and was trained to be a Ju. By his time the rigid distinction between patrician and plebeian had begun to break down. Some of the old noble families, as has been said above, had been wiped out or had survived only as plebeians. On the other hand, some able Ju administrators had gone up in the world. There were good opportunities for an ambitious and talented youngster; but hardly if he was a man with strong ethical principles. That violent bully, Chi Tzu, was at the height of his power when the young Chung-ni was ready to be employed by his betters. It could hardly have been against the will of the Three Han that he got his first very minor post, the wardenship of some public granaries; and he could not have gone on to higher posts, unless they had thought he was at least innocuous to their interests. Nevertheless, when the poor duke had to flee for his life, Chung-ni went into voluntary exile.

By this time he was becoming known, not only as a

hard-working and loyal civil servant, but also as a real expert in that other branch of Ju expertise, namely the hundred and one details of the time-honoured rituals. Obviously, here was a man of outstanding ability, since he could combine both branches of learning, and, when called in to advise on some knotty point in ritual or administration, could be relied on to illuminate the problem. Some time or other he carried out a long-cherished plan and went to the Chou capital, and examined there the evidences of the Chou order of government from the beginning; and all the time his reverence for the great Duke Chou became deeper and deeper. Thus, in those troubled days, serious-minded men began to gather round him, seeing in him a man who knew the saving traditions of happier times.

When the new duke succeeded and Chi Tzu at last died, Chung-ni's services were again required, and a career of honour stretched before him. Things were better in the country. The leaders of the Three Han seem to have realized that public opinion, within and without the country, was against their overweening arrogance, and that it had better be placated. Thus, Chung-ni was able, without truckling to the bad elements in high places, to go up the ladder of state service. His name may well have been in men's mouths as likely to be ennobled as a *ta fu*. Young men who wanted to learn the principles and technique of official life set themselves to school with him. We have to discount the extravagant claims of later devotees, that whilst the 'Master' was *ssu-k'ou* (chief of police and punisher of crime) bad men dared not come to the capital, and, if a man dropped something precious in the road, he was sure to regain it. But there is no reason for doubting that he used his power to do justly and to love mercy. So also, when acting as plenipotentiary in interstate politics, he stood firmly, not only for the traditional rituals of official intercourse, but also for the ethical principles which underlay them, and which to him were the linch-pin of the Great Society (*t'ien hsia*).

He is recorded as having said: 'At fifteen I set my mind on

learning, at thirty I stood firm, at forty I knew my own mind, at fifty I recognized Heaven's commission . . .' It was when he was nearing his fiftieth year that there was suddenly an end to all this prosperity. According to the accounts—and they may be suspected of dramatizing a process of growing disillusionment—Lu State's neighbours and rivals, being concerned at its rise from weakness to strength, successfully debauched the duke and his intimates by the present of some very seductive singing girls. Chung-ni, the duke's *ssu-k'ou*, resigned from his office and left the country with those of his followers who remained faithful to him. For eighteen years he was an exile, in the first instance a voluntary one, and inspired by the sense that he had made his protest whatever the cost. But year after year went past and no move was made to recall him. One of the Three Han leaders on his death-bed warned his clan to such effect that, although some of his followers were welcomed back and given posts, the man who had trained them was rigorously kept in exile.

During those years Chung-ni experienced great vicissitudes of fortune. On the one hand, his reputation had spread abroad, and this lord and the other were curious to meet him and hear what he had to say on the principles and practice of good government. On the other hand, the arrival of the little group of exiles at the border of a state was the signal for acts of suspicion and hostility. There were times when they were in danger of their lives, and their leader had to encourage the faint-hearted with the assurance that he had a divine commission to fulfil. There were times when they had to break up their fellowship and 'the Master' himself went short of food. One lesson of these eighteen years was that there was not a single duke or lord who was prepared to make the experiment of governing by those guiding principles of his, man-to-man-ness (*jen*), long-sighted planning in all state business (*chih*), unfailing fidelity to one's word (*hsin*), and trust in Providence and the common people to prove by their support that right is right and wrong is wrong.

Finally, when he was an old man, he was invited back with honour to his native land. He apparently made no effort to enter the State service again: very likely he was not encouraged to do so. He settled down as a private teacher: the first private teacher in the history of China, and the father of that amazing line of private teachers who, from that day to this, have taught that unless a man is prepared to learn to do right he cannot be regarded as fully a man. There was a second way in which Chung-ni proved himself a great innovator. He welcomed as his students men of peasant stock and men from other States. For seven years the Master continued to fulfil his divine commission among them. Then he died, at the age of seventy-two: in the eyes of his countrymen full of years and honour, in his own eyes a failure. The convictions which he had tried to inculcate had not been accepted as more than ideals, than principles which were, doubtless, practicable in golden ages of the past, but could not be expected to work in the world as it was then.

What Confucius Taught

Among the Han Dynasty scholars there was one school, a markedly superstitious one, which regarded this K'ung Chung-ni as the prophet who had taught an abandoned age the judgments of Heaven. They professed to be inspired by him to the discovery of a science of omens, by which the righteous were encouraged in the straight way and the wicked were warned of what lay in store for them. Another school, more intelligent and therefore less superstitious, regarded him mainly as the arch-statesman who had discovered the eternal principles of right government. This was government by moral example and the force of gratitude: a whole people loving to obey their admirable guardians whose commands brought such great benefits to them. This school became the very much more powerful of the two. Then in Sung times and after, there was the Ch'eng-Chu interpretation of the Sage as primarily a philosopher, uniquely wise as to the order of the universe and man's place in it. As such he must be assumed as knowing the truth about everything; and if he had not made himself clear at all points, were there not these later teachers who had so brilliantly systematized the original deposit of truth?

Thus each school of thought emphasized one aspect of their great Master's teaching to the exclusion of the other aspects, and by their dogmatism tended to make his liberating power an enslavement of the soul. As we examine this teaching to-day, it seems to rise above these limitations; and, if to our minds he appears at times to be profoundly conservative, defending the lost cause of a decaying feudalism, we can also see that he did this under the conviction that the spirit and forms of Duke Chou's social order gave men a better chance of true human relations. In this sense he was a social reformer, as has been maintained often enough in this twentieth century of ours; although it is clear that he had in the forefront of his mind the individual who makes the society, not the society which makes the individual. Our modern principles of political democracy would doubtless have horrified him. And yet, as has been noted above, he was the first to welcome plebeians into his intimate circle of disciples.

We have to recapture, as far as we can, the mind of a man in a society still impregnated with the old tribal limitations of consciousness and modes of thought:[1] for feudalism is an emergent form of tribalism. In a tribal society the individual is largely sunk in the mass of his fellows. He uses the processes of reason in simple ways—since he can measure and count—but not self-consciously. He is only doing what everybody else is doing: and that is reason enough for him. Then some great outward changes come to his life. Society is torn from its customary moorings. A new type of individual emerges, one who fears neither gods nor men: the rank individualist, as we call him. That was the stage in Chinese history when Confucius was born and came to examine his own country of Lu and the Great Society of the Chou States. The Chi Tzus of his world were

[1] Cp. F. M. Cornford, *From Religion to Philosophy* (1912) Ch. I—III.

his problem, the men who were apparently bigger persons because they felt free to indulge their lust and were able to enforce their will on other men.

Something in Confucius—he himself attributed it to Heaven and the example of Duke Chou—made him deny real personality to these men and to persist, in spite of his age turning its back on him, in his affirmation that a real man is quite other. Thus he took the old concept of *jen* (the good fellow, the good clansman), and he made of it something radically different. A *jen* man was one who saw his fellow man, whatever his station, as just as much of a man as himself, as just as much entitled to life and happiness. Confucius took the current term *chun tzu* (a nobleman) and said a man was not a nobleman unless he was a noble man. By teaching this, and, what is more, by living it, Confucius discovered the individual to himself on a new level of self-consciousness. In this we can see 'the Sage' using his reason in profoundly direct fashion, so that we may well call him a philosopher in one sense. In another sense, however, he was not. He did not use his reason systematically to examine every question about man's life and the life of the universe. He arrived at his basic conclusions more by instinctive acts of faith in man and the order of the universe.

There were two chief ways in which he showed that he had a sound command of the tool of self-conscious reasoning. In the first place, as a member of the professional class of the Ju, the men who had the duty of recording events as they happened, he conducted a campaign for speaking the truth, the exact truth, neither more nor less. If the heir to a dukedom killed his father and yet became duke, the official annalist must put it on record that he was guilty of the supremely inhuman crime of patricide. If a lord had, by his oppression, goaded his people beyond all bearing, then the killing of him was not to be recorded as the atrocious crime of regicide; although for a high official to head the plot was reprehensible as it was not for the common people: he had sworn vows of loyalty and had the option of retiring from a position which compromised him. In the second place, Confucius had his doubts about the kind of religiousness he saw in every court about him. The ethical filial piety, for example, which seemed to him to have inspired Duke Chou's actions, that he admired beyond measure. But when a good old lord died and the sons who had plagued him alive proceeded to give him the most colossal funeral, draining the resources of the country to show how pious they were and what big fellows they were in the world, or perhaps to make sure that the ghosts of their ancestors should not plague them, that did not strike Confucius as religion. If they could not serve their father alive, how could they serve him when he was dead? Yet to maintain, as the tendency in modern times is, that Confucius discounted religion as a whole, would seem to be a real misapprehension. The man who said 'The wicked one has no one he can pray to,' and who was buoyed up in his exile by the conviction that he had a commission from Heaven, and therefore could not have his life snuffed out by a gang of border roughs, that man was not irreligious in the full rationalist sense. Again we have to try and recapture the religious stage which Chinese society had reached at that time. Tribal religion, with its emphasis on the common ritual act as the essence, has its own scheme of ethical requirements; but the moral reason works there on a patently low level. Confucius, with his sense of a High Heaven ordering the universe on a moral basis, and with his inclusion of all men of whatever tribe as equal humans with equal rights, was no enemy of high religion.

There we must leave him. The detailed treatment of his teaching is to be found in standard works on him. The reason why his life has occupied our attention more than his tenets is because there is reason for believing that unless he had sacrificed his career and stuck unflinchingly to his vision of man, he could not have become to his fellow countrymen and the peoples of Korea, Japan, and Indo-China a sage who had the saving truth in him. So vast an influence requires some explanation.

Confucius's Disciples and the Rise of Mohism

The Master is recorded as saying that only one of his disciples really understood him: and he died prematurely. The other disciples seem to have varied very much. We have intimate sidelights on them, because their master's method in education plainly was to stimulate them to ask questions; and a large number of these questions are in the *Analects*. So also are certain pithy comments which their master made about the men who professed loyalty to his principles. As for that loyalty, some of them must have had it to a high degree—within the measure of each man's comprehension of his teacher. Thus, for example, one Tseng Ts'an, whom later ages came to regard as the author of the main part of *The Great Learning*, was a most devoted adherent. Yet, if we put together all the stories about Tseng and what he taught, he was a consummate filial-pietist. He exalted fathers and mothers to the position of gods in relation to their sons and daughters-in-law, as may be judged by the story of him on his death-bed. He gave orders that he should be stripped naked in order that he might demonstrate that he had kept the charge and gave back the perfect body which his parents had bestowed on him at birth. Even while he was learning from his master —according to the *Analects*—this tendency was quite marked in him. And yet, taking the *Analects* as a whole, Confucius was not a filial-pietist in that extreme sense. Later ages came to believe that he was, and that in his day this was the universally accepted position, from the point of view of historians to-day very dubiously true. We see, therefore, how in this matter Tseng Ts'an was victorious over his master in his appeal to the religious instincts of the Chinese people.

The reliable books have very little to say about what the seventy odd intimate disciples did after Confucius's death. Apparently some held posts in the state service, others became tutors to young lordlings, others perhaps retired into private life to become teachers in their home neighbourhood. A few, we conjecture on the basis of general probability and a statement in the *Record of History* (second century B.C.), stayed by their master's tomb for some years; and perhaps it was these who wrote down their recollections and so started the book which afterwards became that very composite work, the *Analects*. All we can say confidently is that something of immense import had happened in the Great Society. On the one hand, there came to be in all the courts men who were prone to decide a moral issue on the basis of 'the Master said.' Sooner or later there were teachers in the different States who possessed each a copy of one or two books which the Master had commended. Chief among these books was the *Book of Songs* which he had sedulously used for instruction, and the songs in which it is quite likely that he had selected. There was also the *Yi Scriptures* (*Book of Changes*) which, in spite of the traditional belief, we may regard as not having had any particular appeal to Confucius. These teachers handed on to their disciples their expositions (*ch'uan*) of these sacred works, and here, again, when questions arose as to what was right and what wrong, the answer would be given: 'The Master said . . .' Very likely the maxim given was only very approximately what the Master had said or would have said. In any case, the Great Tradition grew and sank more and more into men's hearts.

The Ju as a class were becoming more numerous and better educated. They must always have had a certain standard of professional honour and mutual loyalty. As the years went on, this became bound up with loyalty to the greatest of their fraternity, Confucius. And then, in the fourth and third centuries, it became the fashion for successful potentates, kings as they were, in reality if not in name, to collect well-known men of learning together, house them and feed them, and encourage them to discuss principles of government and ethics and ritual. At these centres old books were collected, and new books, or expansions of the old, came to be written. Thus the different versions of Confucius's teaching were preserved and amplified, and we may suppose that *The Mean-in-action* and *The Great Learning* came in for their share of attention.

On the other hand, this remarkable something which had happened to the people of North China extended far beyond the direct influence of Confucius. In spite of almost continual warfare in one part or another of that region, there was an amazing uprush of intellectual vitality. During the three centuries, the fifth to the third B.C., every sort of question came to be asked about man and the universe, and a rich variety of theory was advanced. By the end of the fourth century, the people in the direct tradition of Confucius's teaching were quite old-fashioned. So also were the followers of the second great teacher, Mo Ti, who came one to two generations after Confucius. Since this school is important both for its own sake and because the final sections of *The Great Learning* look very like a denunciation of Mohist principles, we must examine them in some detail.

Mo Ti and his chief disciple, Ch'in Hua-li, owed a great deal of their inspiration in the first instance to Confucius. When, however, Mo Ti's teaching got well into its stride, it tended more and more away from the Confucianist position. It is rather a surprising phenomenon to us to-day, because, whereas in England the combination of strong religious beliefs and a utilitarian ethic came only in the eighteenth century, China saw this combination right back in the early days of its intellectual history. Mo Ti was a staunch supporter of the old religion. To him Heaven and Earth, the nature deities, and the ancient sage-kings unquestionably existed and exercised the decisive influence in human affairs. Indeed, we may say, since he had a profoundly logical mind, his position was that they must exist: otherwise society would collapse. He had a trenchant prophetic power about him, denounced the evils of society without mincing matters, and in doing so was able to use a gift of sarcasm with devastating effect. We find again and again in the *Book of Mo Tzu*, of which the greater part has survived to the present, most striking examples of the logical device of *reductio ad absurdum*. He used this weapon, of course, against those in authority who, in his eyes, were responsible for the miseries to be found in every State. 'You lords and gentlemen of this world,' he says with sardonic force, 'regard yourselves as immensely clear as to your own interests, and yet these perpetual wars in which you engage are glaringly opposed to those interests.' In other words, they were not only wicked, provoking the just wrath and indignation of Heaven, but also incredibly silly.

No teacher, perhaps, in all Chinese history has quite equalled Mo Ti in his whole-hearted and sacrificial love of the common people. He fought in the cause of their welfare on all occasions. For their sakes he condemned, not all warfare, but aggressive warfare, however good the grounds might appear to be. For them he was spurred on to develop his practical genius in making engines for the defence of towns and devising the tactics for this kind of warfare. He also, with his utilitarian mind, took a line which brought him into trouble with the Confucianists in his day and a hundred years later, and, indeed, all down the ages. The type of religion which Tseng Ts'an advocated was beoming more and more prevalent, and it was laid not only on the nobility, but also on the common people that they were guilty of inhuman wickedness if they failed to give their parents elaborate funerals and to endure the rigours of mourning for the prescribed two years and a month. This, said Mo Ti, was not the practice of humanity but the very reverse. So also with the cultivation of the art of music and dancing in the courts. It involved enormous expenditure, took off an immense quantity of potential man-power into unproductive callings, and, at the same time, tempted the leaders of society to waste the time which they should be spending in organizing the food supply and the administration of justice. This, said Mo Ti, is not civilization but barbarism.

We cannot but admire this great-hearted man, and note with sympathetic interest the revival of the study of him in modern China. None the less, he had serious limitations, or rather, was driven by the narrow utilitarian temper of his mind to extraordinary excesses in his political thinking. To him the solution of the political problem was merely one of fearing the judgments of the gods, visualizing in what the true wealth of the country consisted, and then straightway reorganizing government on the basis of achieving unity of effort throughout the community. It was quite simple: find the ablest and the most virtuous men and give them entire control; and inculcate on the common people and each rank in the hierarchy of officials the necessity of finding out what their immediate superiors thought in all practical matters, and then modelling their thoughts precisely in those ways. This fantastically mechanical exercise of reason did not, apparently, shock the people of Mo Ti's age in the way that his denunciation of extravagant funerals did. In fact, the idea of political unity carried to the pitch of uniformity had its influence in Confucian circles. Nevertheless the verdict of history has been made by one shrewd Taoist critic some two to three hundred years later. He said: 'Mo Ti did not understand human nature.' The best Confucianist minds, for their part, fastened on his exaltation of profit as his most dangerous doctrine. Once allow this principle, they said, and every class in society will pursue its own idea of profit, and this will bring the downfall of society. They urged what we call to-day 'values' in contrast with utilities, Confucius's virtues of *jen* (man-to-manness), and *yi* (righteousness). The fostering of these was the end of government. The significant thing is that a little over a hundred years after Mo Ti there arose a school of hard-headed realist thinkers who took this utilitarian logic and the idea of simplifying society, and made a political philosophy of it which would have shocked Mo Ti to the bottom of his soul.

Mohism flourished for two hundred years, and Mohists are to be heard of as late as the first century B.C. What little we know about them is attractive for the most part. They organized themselves into congregations under leaders, and stories of them reveal a spirit of simple fidelity to principle. One section, however, of them came to take part in the great game of logic-chopping which sprang up. In this they proved themselves worthy of the great practical logician, their master. They attacked the problems in a serious spirit and drew some very sound conclusions. It is open to conjecture whether a strain of relativity which is to be found in *The Mean-in-action* was not one of the factors which contributed to make these Mohists and other intellectualists of their day explore the meaning and scope of 'knowledge.'

The Age of Speculation

Plato and Aristotle were the culminating thinkers in an epoch of speculation which started long before them. Confucius and Mo Ti came at the beginning of the Chinese epoch of speculation. This does not necessarily make them any less important, but it does mean that in their day the art of conscious reasoning and its corollary, the art of prose composition, had not reached the level which they had when Plato and Aristotle began to write. This is very clear when we come to examine the records of Confucius's teaching. We cannot be sure that he did any consecutive writing, whilst what his disciples, after his death, made of the pious duty of writing down their recollections is plain from the *Analects*. There is some slight rudimentary arrangement of materials at certain points, but most of the book is unconnected. We have to assume it had not been discovered in Confucius's time that a man could take a theme and give a consecutive reasoned treatment of it in prose. The only methodical writing was that done by the annalists. However, the time had come for the discovery. Either Mo Ti or his recorders, presumably Mo Ti himself, with his highly logical mind, invented theme composition, for in the book of his teachings he appears as carrying on long arguments of a very dialectical kind.

Confucius's grandson, Tzu Ssu, more or less a contemporary of Mo Ti's and traditionally regarded as the author of *The Mean-in-action*, has to be considered in this connection. *The Mean-in-action* is not an aggressively dialectical work like the famous chapters in the *Book of Mo Tzu*. At first sight it may appear to be much after the pattern of the *Analects*. Closer examination, however, reveals that the first half, at any rate, was written on a well-reasoned plan: the work of a man with an essentially rational mind, though not familiar with the essay form of writing. If, then, Tzu Ssu may be taken as the author, his book is one of the greatest possible significance, namely the earliest we possess to-day of any work written by a really philosophical-minded Chinese. Thus, if Confucius discovered the ethical individual to himself and Mo Ti discovered the dialectically logical individual to himself, then Tzu Ssu discovered the reasoning, metaphysical-minded individual to himself. And when we realize this, we realize also that these three men had disciples. That is to say, when they tried out their ideas on friendly minds there was a response, and by their intercommunication teacher and disciple moved on to a new level of self-conscious thinking.

This marked the point in time when this old semi-tribal society came to the parting of the ways. We may venture on a generalization. Without some individuals in such a society achieving some such powers of more acute self-consciousness, and thereby becoming able to exercise deliberately their faculty of reason, that society cannot go on to be civilized in the full sense. It will either break up or slip back into barbarism, and the world is littered with the remains of cultures which, having arrived at a time of testing, have been inadequate to the challenge. That the forefathers of the Chinese people did not fail when the Chou feudal system broke down is due to the fact that, somehow or other, their culture had enough spiritual power to produce these three men, Confucius, Tsu Ssu, and Mo Ti, and to supply them with disciples who from their teachings made new, creative traditions.

The result was nothing less than the creation of a new type of individual. But, if we are to appreciate the significance of this creation, we must include in our purview the men who came to think in very different fashion to the Confucianists and Mohists. One swallow does not make a summer; and there was sufficient conservatism mixed up with Chung-ni's and Mo Ti's schools of thought for there to be a real danger of premature dogmatism. Confucius was a Ju, and his tenets appealed to the Ju, a class of society which already had its very strong traditions, whilst Mo Ti's appeal was, in part, to simple, unquestioning minds, for he called for faith in the old gods. That the miracle of creation went on and extended its scope must be put down in good measure to the rise of the Taoist intellectualist thinkers, but also to a number of other intellectualists, men of a highly radical turn of mind.

Of recent years there has been very vigorous discussion as to the first beginnings of Taoism. There seems more and more reason for doubting whether the famous *Tao Te Ching* was written by the Lao Tan who was a contemporary of Confucius. The book looks much more like an amalgam of Taoist sentiments current in the fourth century B.C. or even later. If that be taken to be the case, then we have no detailed information as to the views of the first Taoist recluses, the kind of men of whom, for instance, we catch glimpses in the *Analects*. The end of the fourth century is when they emerge into the light of history, and then through the writings under the name of the greatest Taoist thinker of all time, Chuang Chou. In this book we see them as mainly, but by no means exclusively, men who were devoted to the contemplative's manner of life and the contemplative's search for absolute truth. They claimed, indeed, to have solved the riddle of the universe and of man as no Confucianist or Mohist could hope to solve it, busy as those were with temporal things.

All Taoist theories, richly varied though they were, had one basic dogma, that the Tao, the hidden core of reality in the universe, is, on the one hand, utterly indefinable and, on the other, the secret source of true personality in the individual. Thus the individual by the right approach to the Tao may become a channel for its mysterious power, a body of people, a society cannot. For some Taoists this meant that the very existence of society was unnecessary, and even a source of infection for the individual. For others, as in the *Tao te Ching*, the man with the power of the Tao exercised a subtle influence over ordinary people. He led them without them knowing, and, as his influence spread, a simple uncalculating happiness came to the whole community.

So great was the variety of Taoist opinion that later bibliographers have had great doubts how to classify some of the writers of this period. They sometimes call them Taoists and sometimes Ming Chia (Logicians). It was, indeed, an age of untrammelled freedom in speculation. As an instance of the refinement of thought which was achieved, take the following quotation from a very acute critic of somewhere about the third century B.C. It is also significant as showing how some of the distinctive ideas of *The Mean-in-action* penetrated into Taoist circles.

To be public-minded, belonging to no party and ready to change one's opinions; making up one's mind, but not the slave of dogma, and following the trend of things, but not being double-minded; not being too much engaged in contemplation, but not making deliberate efforts after wisdom; not having partialities about men and things, but going with them all equally: of the men of the past who concentrated on these aspects of the art of the Tao there were P'eng Meng, T'ian P'ien, and Shen Tao. They heard the news of the Tao and rejoiced. For them the regular harmony of everything in Nature was the guiding principle. The sky, they said, can cover but not support us; the earth can support but cannot cover us. The Supreme Tao is able to include; it is not able to dissect. These men knew that all things had their possibilities and their impossibilities. Hence, they said, If selections be made, then universality will be lost: if a man sets forth certain principles, then they are not entirely true. The Tao leaves out nothing. Thus it was that Shen Tao said. . . . Knowledge is not knowledge. (*Book of Chuang Tzu*, c. 33.)

The paradoxical mind is seen at work here, using reason

to assail the conclusions of reason. In this age there were plenty who took delight in this, some of them with a sophist's frivolity, searching out all the logical puzzles and paradoxes of experience that they could find. For this reason serious-minded men came to despise them. Chuang Chou, (?369–?286), probably the most brilliant writer that China has produced, was able to beat these sophists at their own game, for he was exquisitely aware of the relativity of reason's conclusions. But he had also a saving sense of humour and a poet's genius for striking to the heart of things. By combining the methods of reason and experience he found a meaning to life for the individual. Politically he was a philosophical anarchist, seeing no value in society at all, and amused at the grotesque compromises into which the Confucianists were decoyed by their desire to make the best of both worlds.

From the ranks of the Confucianists there came, in Chuang Chou's age, only one outstanding figure. This was Mencius, mentioned in more than one record as a follower of Tzu Ssu. Traces of influence by *The Mean-in-action* can be found in Mencius's writings, but not so many as one would expect, if he really were a disciple of Tzu Ssu. The explanation of this may lie in the fact that Mencius was not a metaphysician by temperament but a political philosopher and a psychologist. His chief interest to us in this introduction is in his revolt against a new philosophy of man which was becoming very popular in his time. It was a kind of philosophic Epicureanism, its ethic based on the existence of the natural appetites. To this Mencius's reply was that the essential thing about man is, not his appetites, but a natural aptitude for goodness. This, as we have seen in Chapter I, became a very important part of the Chinese Great Tradition and, in particular, a fundamental dogma of the Confucianist faith. The idea, therefore, has been prevalent in China that Confucius himself believed this. If he did, there is no convincing trace of it in the reliable records of his teaching. The truth probably is that he did not, but that his mind unconsciously tended in that direction. The same applies to *The Mean-in-action* and *The Great Learning* in which we find no overt trace of this theory. We must emphasize again that it was a long time before the Chinese, or even Confucianists generally, came to believe this. The most truly learned and acute Confucianist thinker of the classical era, Hsun Ch'ing (298–238 B.C.), affirmed that man's nature was exactly the reverse: man had a natural aptitude for evil. And in Han times Yang Hsiung was to maintain that the truth lay between the two contentions: man was by nature morally indifferent, and everything depended on what education could do to make the right environment.

Shang Yang the Materialist and Hsun Ch'ing the Humanist

In addition to all these movements the fourth century saw in the westernmost and least civilized of the Chou States the rise of that sinister movement which in Chapter I has been described as totalitarianism. The prime mover in this was Shang Yang, a man with an untiring driving power in affairs of State, and able also to think out a new ethic of the individual and the State. He was a realist in the full sense in which it is popularly—and so unwarrantably—used to-day. He took the Epicurean theory and carried it to its extreme materialistic conclusion. Every man in this world was out for himself, to get as much comfort and security and reputation as he could. Since this meant anarchy and no happiness for any one, it is the State's business to order things with a view to getting the greatest possible happiness for the greatest possible number. This was precisely what Mo Ti had aimed at with his political utilitarianism; although he presupposed a moral order of the universe, which Shang Yang did not. The latter denounced both the vested interests of the old feudal aristocracy and the specious, comfort-making trades of teaching, commerce, innkeeping, and the like as not serving the interests of the whole community. Apart from the work of administration, there were only two essential industries, agriculture and war-making, and the whole man-power of the country must be mobilized for these two services. The State had room for only two kinds of citizens, the docile, law-abiding kind which could be spurred to make two ears of corn grow where there had been only one, and the ambitious, trouble-making kind which could be drafted into the army and there either be expeditiously killed, and so be no more trouble to the State, or be forged by the harsh discipline of war into good tools for the work of administering the country. This work must be carried out on the basis of two principles, One was that the king should make laws which applied to everybody alike, including the king and the royal house: it was vital that there should be unerring justice. The other was that these laws should be the means by which the productive members of society should get rewards for their labours, and the unproductive, the lazy or inefficient people, should be punished. The rewards must be hard to win and the punishments easy to incur. This was Shang Yang's realism, so like to that of Thomas Hobbes of Malmesbury in the seventeenth century. It remains only to add that since the State existed for the greatest happiness of the greatest number, and the rewards of life rightly went to the efficient and the penalties and pains to the inefficient, therefore it followed that that State which had amassed the most food supplies and perfected its war-machine, had the right to war down the less efficient other States. The logic of this conclusion is unassailable, provided that man may rightly be treated on this atomistic, equalitarian basis.

Shang Yang came to a bad end: he was a little too logical for the people of Ch'in State. But there is good ground for believing that Ch'in was organized on this basis and continued to run along these lines: hence its conquest of all the other States three generations later. There is also good evidence to show that a number of men in these other States, both administrators and philosophers, were attracted by this realism. There was a regular school of them, and they came to be known as the Fa Chia (Legalists). The fact that no other State was reorganized in this way does not necessarily mean that they were convinced there was a higher way. Rather it was because the upper classes were too strong for any would-be autocrat. They were not prepared to sacrifice their time-honoured privileges, one of which was that a nobleman had the code of chivalry to keep him straight and was not to be made subject to the Law: that was for keeping the common people in order. This idea of *noblesse oblige* is very conspicuous in *The Great Learning*, and, as we shall see in Chapter IV, it is quite likely that this book was written in the face of Shang Yang's materialistic realism.

It is significant that Hsun Ch'ing, good Confucianist and able analyser as he was, should have a distinct touch of the legalist about him. He had no pretty illusions about human nature in the raw. He was profoundly convinced of the need for law and order, for, he said, man's desires are limitless, the means for satisfying them strictly limited. The individual, therefore, must be educated to be satisfied in that station in life in which he finds himself. Hsun Ch'ing is important for this introduction for three reasons. First, there is his conviction that man has a natural aptitude for evil. Second, he believed whole-heartedly in a moral order of the universe, but man had no extraneous, miraculous aids to the good life, as for example, spectacular judgments from Heaven: man had got to save himself. Third, he believed that the means for this salvation existed, partly through the shining example of the Sages, men who had toilfully mastered their desires and built up the power of personality in themselves, partly through education in the noble community-rites which had been handed down and which made for basic social cohesion. Thus for him education was more than mere book learning. It was the disciplining of private lust through great sacraments of daily life. By these the individual's true self, an acquired self fostered by habit, came into flower. Man fulfilled his end by practising the poetry of the five Heaven-established relationships: father and son, prince and minister, elders and juniors, husband and wife, and friend and friend. This was another type of realism than that which the Legalists advocated.

It is difficult to overestimate Hsun Ch'ing's influence in ancient China. In so many respects he was the fine flower of Ju philosophy. It is almost certain that many of the works which make up the great *Record of Ritual*, in which *The Mean-in-action* and *The Great Learning* were preserved, were written by disciples of his. And this great compendium quickly won its way to canonical status. In it a number of passages can be found which are word-for-word quotations from Hsun Ch'ing's writings. Yet his own writings never achieved canonical status. Was he, by any chance, too deistic in his views of 'Heaven' or too rationalistic in his view of man? These are questions which may well be asked.

CHAPTER IV

WHO WROTE 'THE MEAN-IN-ACTION' AND 'THE GREAT LEARNING'?

IN this chapter the reader is to come face to face with the authors of these two books. Since it must be assumed that he is not concerned with the details of historical criticism, these are cut to the barest possible minimum, and what are given serve the extra purpose of illustrating the particular mentality of each author. After all, to read an old book intelligently involves having some idea whether the man who wrote it thought in much the same way that we do, and had a language that enabled him to express himself more or less precisely.

To the question, Who wrote *The Mean-in-action*? the answer is that we cannot be sure. The uniform tradition has been that Tsu Ssu, grandson of Confucius, wrote it. But the external evidence for this is not very good, whilst the occurrence in one section of the book of certain phrases and ideas which are naturally attributable to the age of the First Emperor (mid third century B.C.) brings the whole book under suspicion of being much later than the middle of the fifth century. One recent theory [1] is that the whole of the latter half of the book, beginning with the words in Legge's c. 20: 'When those in inferior positions . . .' is the work of a man who belonged to the Mencius section of the Confucianist school and who lived either in the First Emperor's time or later in Han times. Excellent as this theory is in many ways, there are difficulties attached

---

[1] This theory is put forth by Professor Feng Yu-lan, Ph.D., in his *Chung Kuo Che Hsüeh Shih*, 1931. An English translation of this work has been made by Prof. Derk Bodde, Ph.D., *A History of Chinese Philosophy*, Peiping, 1937 (also London, Allen & Unwin). This book is indispensable for any one wishing to make a close study of early Chinese philosophy.

to it. I venture to propose some alterations which seem to me to avoid those difficulties.

Using A to denote the original author, and B to denote his amplifier, I divide the text as follows:

C. 1., author B. (In this I follow Dr. Feng Yu-lan.)

C. 2 to the end of Legge's c. 26, par. 6, author A.

Legge's c. 26, par. 7 to the end of Legge's c. 31, author B.

Legge's c. 32, author A. In the original work this chapter follows the first half of Legge's c. 26, par. 6.

Legge's c. 33 to the end, author B.

I accept Confucius's grandson, Tzu Ssu, as author A. Author B was a Confucianist of the First Emperor's time.

The Great Learning also is a problem. The pre-Sung scholars have no theory which need occupy our attention. Nor does Chu Hsi's suggestion of Confucius as responsible for the opening section and Tseng Ts'an, the filial pietist, for the rest, command any respect to-day. The critical scholar really has to start from scratch and do the best he can from internal evidence. My own position is that it was the work of an unkown Confucianist just before the time of Mencius, and that Ch'eng Yi-ch'uan and Chu Hsi were wrong in rearranging the text as they did.

The reasons for these new suggestions will appear as we go on. The argument falls into three parts. First, the language of the two books has been subjected to the closest scrutiny, and comparison made with the language of books which we can date with confidence. Second, the two books have been explored with a view to discovering what it was that the authors were particularly stirred to say. Third, the external evidence has been sifted. I would commend this order to the student of any such problem, adding only that when he has satisfied himself that he has discovered the book's 'great idea,' he should go back to his notes on the language and re-examine them in the light of what he has discovered in the second stage of the inquiry.

The Language of 'The Mean-in-action' and 'The Great Learning'

For the sake of brevity the two books are taken together. A very great deal might be written on the language questions which arise in their connection, but the main points which emerge can be treated under the following four headings: (1) Changes in the meaning of certain key terms, either nouns or verbs.[1] (2) Developments in ethical discernment as seen in the terms for virtues and vices. (3) Development of precision of thought and range of reasoning as seen in the grammatical expressions used to denote causation and inference. (4) The same development in relation to expressions used to denote comparison.

(1) That remarkable changes in language should have come in this epoch (the sixth to the third century B.C.) is only to be expected considering the immense intellectual excitement which has been described in Chapter III. *T'ien* (Heaven) obviously was susceptible to reinterpretation when the rational mind got to work. Thus in Hsun Tzu's book (third century B.C.) Heaven denotes what is often described as the Law of Nature. But to the poets of the *Book of Songs* and to the Confucius of the *Analects*, *T'ien* is the great overruling Providence with a Will demanding righteousness from man, bringing good fortune to the virtuous and evil fortune to the wicked. For us the landmark here is Mencius, in whose book both meanings occur. In the A sections of *The Mean-in-action* we find the earlier view, in the B sections there is no sign of it. In *The Great Learning* the earlier view prevails.

Tao, which meant originally a road or the head set forward in travelling, came in time to be used metaphorically for a way of knowledge and virtue and mastery of life generally. Conservative scholars would insist that the 'Way' was that marked out by the high ancestors for their descendants to follow, but the new minds of our epoch

[1] In an ideographic language there is no modification of a concept-stem in order to make clear that the concept is being expressed as a name or an action or a modifier. Thus, an ideograph may be at once a noun and a verb and an adjective, etc.

claimed that what they discovered by process of reasoning or mystical illumination was *tao*. Indeed, each would say that his system was *the tao*. By the fourth century B.C. almost any sort of principle was being called a *tao*. In the A sections of *The Mean-in-action*, *tao* is used very much as it is in the *Analects*, that is sparingly, for some great way of life opening out to view, or the Great Way of Heaven. *The Great Learning* is somewhat more free in its use, e.g. in the last section of it we find: 'For the creation of wealth there is a great *tao*.'

Te—perhaps the most fascinating of all Chinese words—seems to have started life meaning the magic power, either beneficent or malicious, which was exercised by any extraordinary individual, man or thing, e.g. a weird-shaped mountain or a great river. Then in the new age it can be found in relation to the corrupting influence of a great villain, but predominantly it denotes the individual power in some great personality, and so spiritual power, moral power, and so outstanding virtue. In the third century *tao* and *te* are found put together, apparently having no more meaning than principled goodness. In our two books *te* has not reached that stage. In both its meaning seems to hover between power of personality and moral power, about the stage of meaning it had reached in the *Analects*.

Chih (to know) has to be examined with particular care. Confucius emphasized the duty to know, and apparently for him the way to know was to learn. That sounds too elementary to be noted. But the question is, to learn what? With him it is, perhaps, clear, e.g. the *Songs*, the *Annals of the States*, notes for those in charge of sacrifices; but it is by no means entirely clear in the Confucianist books of this epoch. That is the case with the A sections of *The Mean-in-action*; and if it were not for evidence of a great interest in ritual in that part of the book, we should be at a loss. However, there is that interest, and the absence of any use of that notable fourth- and third-century noun, knowledge or wisdom. Nor, except in a rudimentary sense, does the word *pien* (to distinguish by dialectic) occur. *Pien* was a very popular word in those later centuries. As for *The Great Learning*, there is emphasis on the duty to know as much as one can, and the old-established *chih* is used as a noun; but there is no sign of the later words beloved of the sophists.

Cheng and *ch'ih* in post-Confucian times are both used to denote governing; but the *Analects* and other books show that *cheng*, to keep or put people and things right in the community, was the original word. *Ch'ih*, which comes in the *Book of Songs*[1] and *Analects* as a general word for getting things levelled or systematized, was used by Mo Ti for governing, and both in that and later books it is the common word: a state had to have systematic government or it could not survive. *The Mean-in-action* (A sections) has both words, *The Great Learning* only *ch'ih*.

(2) In the *Book of Songs* there is a rather surprisingly large number of terms for denoting virtues and vices, some of them making quite subtle distinctions. On examination they convey the impression that the basis of distinction between good and bad is either one of *fas* and *nefas*, of what immemorial custom had recognized, or one of instinctive like or dislike on the part of an individual when he realizes that he is being treated well or ill. It is, of course, the kind of thing we should expect from poets in a feudal semi-tribal society. In such a society the good clansman was a good man, and the good man was a good clansman, and ordinary people thought no more about it, until unhappy changes forced them to think. And it is not until we come to the Confucius of the *Analects* that we find an individual vigorously using his moral reason in the full sense. After him ethical intelligence comes more and more into play, and by the fourth century B.C. the great game of defining words had come to stay. In consequence ever finer ethical distinctions came to be made, and in the third century B.C. books we find the practice of putting two words together. So when we find in a certain later section of *The Mean-in-*

---

[1] The *Book of Songs* is the excellent title given by Mr. Arthur Waley in his book on what has generally been known as the *Classic of Odes*.

action an elaborate list of such double-barrelled virtues, we draw the natural conclusion. *The Great Learning* shows traces of the defining habit of mind; but, on the whole, its ethical outlook is both simple, in fact, a little old-fashioned, and yet at the same time impregnated with the new Confucianist universalization of the old semi-tribal code.

(3) The hall mark of the new reasoning mind as seen in Confucius and his successors is its use of *ku* and *tse*, both of them having the force of the conjunction of western grammar. Before these minds got to work *ku* and *tse*, as found in the *Book of Songs*, were used with the force of nouns, the one meaning important affair or affairs, the other a pattern. Then with the enlightenment came the need for expressing the causal connection between events. Event A happened, and as a result (*ku*) event B happened. *Tse*, on the other hand, is illustrated by 'if A, then B, according to the pattern in my mind' (? the pattern of reason). That process of thought is what we call making an inference and is very different from seeing the effect of a cause. It involves a hypothesis, sometimes expressed by the *yü* character at the beginning of the first sentence; and the second sentence has the force not of a statement of fact, but of a conclusion in reason which may not be substantiated by present experience but is ideally true. The distinction between the two terms is very well brought out by two developments. One was introduced by Mo Ti, who, when he wanted to state a general conclusion, introduced it with '*ku yueh*' or *ku wo yueh*, 'therefore I affirm.' Thinkers of every school came to use this *ku yueh*, very often in an impersonal way, 'therefore it is affirmed.' The other development, to be seen particularly in third century B.C. books, was the practice of leaving out *tse* altogether; in other words, in the discussion of practised logicians, the inference was clear from the nature of the statements, so the introductory particle was left out.

In our two books *ku* and *tse* occur continually, but *ku yueh* occurs in *The Great Learning* and in the B part of *The Mean-in-action*, not in the A part. In the B part also we have an example of *tse* being left out. In the A part it is scrupulously used to introduce each inference. *The Great Learning* is specially interesting, because it makes very little use of *tse*. It favours the really old-fashioned *erh hou* (afterwards) to introduce the result, and *pi* (for certain) in the middle of the sentence. This usage occurs occasionally in the sophists' works, and there, as elsewhere, for the most part in a religious connection. Thus *erh*, *hou*, and *pi* all appear to be characteristic of the religious mind.

Another development is traceable with *so yi*, which in the earlier books always denotes 'the means by which.' Then, as time went on, it was used apart from human beings and the means they used to achieve their ends. It denoted also the process by which . . . and in this connection we note that Mencius (end of fourth century) in speaking of causes says sometimes *wu t'a* (for no other cause). These refinements demonstrate much greater precision of thought and expression in relation to causation and process. In *Mencius* also comes *so yi*, used to express identity and essence, e.g. that which constitutes A as A: a usage which reminds us of Aristotle on his characteristic war-path of analysis. This last usage occurs in the B part of *The Mean-in-action*. In the A part it does not occur, but the meaning of 'process by which' does. In *The Great Learning* neither occurs. When the author wants to express process he uses the metaphor of root (*pen*) and branches (*mo*). Also when he wants to say 'consists in,' as in the opening sentence of the book, he says, with admirable simplicity, 'in' (*tsai*).

(4) Since the art of reasoning to any degree involves some power of comparing this object with that, and since primitive man could hardly have survived at all unless he had been able to compare himself with other beings stronger or more speedy than he was, therefore we may feel confident that expressions denoting comparison appear quite early in a language. That, however, does not mean that such expressions would show any very developed power of discrimination in comparing. An early society could go a long way in developing and refining its culture without

being stirred to make more than quite simple classifications such as putting like next to like in one's mind and coining a generic word for them. In the *Book of Songs* the expressions for comparison, *yü*, *jo*,[1] *yu*, and *shih*, do not lend themselves to more than vague resemblances. The poets of these three hundred and fifteen poems had the authentic poetic gift of seizing upon vivid similes,[2] but they were not concerned with making clear the extent of likeness between a simile and the thing it described. Nor, apparently, did they have any clear idea of using an imaginary occurrence to describe an actual one. The Confucius of the *Analects* was able to do this. He illustrated his theories in this way, and he had a special phrase, *pi* or *pi yü* (by way of illustration), for introducing the sentence. *Yu*,[3] too, is seen in the *Analects* to be taking on a more precise meaning, 'equivalent to . . .' There is evidence also that the two commonest terms, *yü* and *jo*, came then and later to be distinguished along the lines of 'as if' and 'like'; a very important distinction, the one expressing a somewhat fanciful comparison, the other an actual likeness.

These usages occur in *The Mean-in-action* (both parts), but are not, with the exception of *yü* and *jo*, part of the author's style in *The Great Learning*. As to the fourth and fifth centuries' passion for defining and classifying with meticulous accuracy, the only signs of this in connection with comparison are in the B sections of *The Mean-in-action*.

[1] *Yü* and *jo* figure prominently in Professor Karlgren's admirable study, *On the Authenticity and Nature of the Tso Chuan* (Göteborg, 1926), but from a different angle of study. The book is invaluable for language studies of this kind, as also are the Harvard-Yenching series of Indexes. Cp. also Professor Duyvendak's *The Book of Lord Shang* (London, 1928), p. 151 et seq.

[2] A good example of this is 'backbone' (*chi*) used by one poet to express logical connection: 'I cry aloud these words: there is *lun* (a binding thread) to them, there is *chi* (a backbone) to them.'—Legge, *Chinese Classics*, Vol. IV, Pt. II, Bk. iv, ode 8. *Lun* came later to denote the great binding relationships of mankind. With this example before us we may conjecture that mankind owes much to its poets in learning to express logical connection.

[3] Cp. F. M. Cornford, *From Religion to Philosophy*, p. 132. The question of 'likeness' originating in 'blood-kinship' is one requiring examination, e.g. has the *pü* (woman) component in *ju* (like) anything to do with matrilinear descents?

The interesting and significant thing is that author A clearly went a good step farther than Confucius in examining below the surface of things, in contrasting appearance and reality. But nowhere do we find in the A part the expression so common in the later writers, 'the *wei* (exterior) . . . the *nei* (interior) . . .' Now in *The Great Learning* this contrast is made in more than one passage with the facility of long practice. Clearly it was a part of the current coin of Confucianist thought by the time the book was written.

To sum up on these four headings, the evidence from language points very definitely to the conclusion that both works were products of an age before the sophists really got to work, and, of course, after Confucius, i.e. somewhere between 450 and 300 B.C. But when we ask which of the two books was prior to the other, the evidence becomes conflicting. Some language features of *The Great Learning* point to its being the later work, others to its being the earlier, and we have to look elsewhere for more decisive evidence.

The Purpose behind 'The Mean-in-action'

Pan Ku, the historian of the First Han Dynasty, had the idea that in Chou times no book was written except under the aegis of some state department. Although he was undoubtedly wrong with regard to the writings of the last three centuries of that era, yet he was right in a sense with regard to earlier times. Roughly speaking, the only people who knew how both to read and write were the Ju, and they were all in some lord's service. What they wrote was either annals or notes on ritual or on divination. Then came Confucius, and his disciples developed a new style of writing, the *ching* composition, i.e. the recorded sayings of a teacher. It was, as the reader will remember, Mo Ti or his disciples who started dealing with one subject at a time in composition.

The significance of this for us here is that our two books

are each a combination of the *ching* form and the *lun* (essay) form. Certainly the author (or authors) of *The Mean-in-action* had something to say on a very definite subject, and the same is true of the author of *The Great Learning*, though his subject was of considerably wider scope.

We will take *The Mean-in-action* first and trace the course of the argument. The first chapter, in some ways an introduction, in others an appreciation, is so clearly the work of a later hand that we need not trouble with it here. Then there comes a series of quotations from Confucius, all dealing with aspects of the *chung* (the mean) or *chung-yung* (the mean-in-action). Plainly our author is concerned about a true way for man, and this way for him is a middle way. Then he begins to use his own words, and what he emphasizes is that this Way is the same for the peasant man or woman as for the nobleman and the sage. The former can start in the Way, the latter can never exhaust its possibilities.

This was certainly worth saying in the days in which this thinker lived. But to prove his point he makes a statement which is just as remarkable, if not more so. It is that vast as the sky and earth are, yet they stop somewhere, but man's questing mind can go beyond these material limits. With regard to supreme greatness or, at the other end of the scale, supreme smallness, the world of the Great Society does not exhaust their possibilities.

Having for a moment broken into the field of metaphysics, the author goes on to expound this common and inexhaustible Way for all men. It is discernible in the finite duties of daily life and in the infinite implications of a solemn religious sacrifice, impalpable spirit being just as real (*ch'eng*) as human beings. From this he passes to the heroes of antiquity. They were persons, each having more power of personality (*te*) than the ordinary man; and it was because they had this outstanding power that by the Will of Heaven they came to be kings and rulers. Further, the really great man's influence does not cease with his death, as is seen in the case of King Wen. He was son to the great Wang Chi, and father to the great King Wu and (even greater) Duke Chou. Thus came the Chou order of civilization with its basic rituals, the worship of Shang Ti (God) and the worship of ancestors.

A philosopher, this man, in our western classical sense. He passes from ethics to metaphysics and then to history, for his *Mean-in-action* must be put to the test of past experience. Now he considers it in relation to right government. Again he uses the argument from history. The great Chou order of civilization depended for its existence not only on its founders, but on the men who were entrusted with the task of making it work. With the right men, the men of the Way, it worked, without them it did not. And the right men were those who had the universal qualities of character essential for the common man as for the great king. Among these filial piety stands highest, for the man who is not filial is a man whom no one can trust, and without trust no government can exist.

So our philosopher comes back to ethics, this time to the religious individual, the filial son. He then maintains that without sincerity in self-examination, no man can be filial, and to achieve this sincerity a man must understand the Good and be real (*ch'eng*) in himself. But *ch'eng*-ness (reality) is the characteristic of Heaven. What, then, about reality in man? It is man's characteristic to be on the way to being real.

From this point on, the argument is concerned with expounding the nature of *ch'eng*-ness, and so demonstrating the vital importance of this quality of reality, whether in man or in 'things.' It is a metaphysical argument, although the author does not lose sight of the common man with his stupidity and weakness. Suddenly, however, we come on a second passage of extraordinary philosophical interest. The author states that effectual reality in man must be continuous, and he draws the conclusion that there is no limit to its continuity. To prove this he boldly brings it into relation with the world of space and time. He sees space as limited by the heavens above and the earth beneath: but the addition of time to the continuum introduces the element of infinity. From this he dares the paradox that reality in man cannot be seen and yet is visible, does not move and yet produces changes, is not active and yet completes. Thus it is like Heaven, unfathomable.

So far, there seems no break in the argument, and at various points there is corroborative evidence of its all coming from the mind of one man.[1] But at this point a change is noticeable. What this change is we shall examine in a moment. First we must note that later another section begins with the same words which introduce an earlier one on reality in man being the means by which all the possibilities in men and things can be realized. In this second passage reality is set forth as the essential quality which makes civilization. The passage ends with a burst of lyrical fervour over the human-heartedness, the unfathomable profundity, the heavenly all-embracingness of this reality in man. It seems to me that this might have been written by our philosopher.

Thus, to put it in three sentences, the great idea which insisted on being set forth in all its implications was that what Confucius had taught about a functioning centrality to life as man's guide, this was true, as practically true for an ignorant peasant as it was inexhaustibly true for the wisest of men. This functioning centrality in life, this mean-in-action, is the very reality of the universe, the mysterious something which is self-propelling, and the secret of all achievement both in human personality and in the growth and development of things, and so the link which makes a partnership between Heaven and Earth and man. Since man's thoughts can reach beyond the material, therefore this mysterious something, in spite of its functioning in space and time, must be distinguished from the material and be regarded as supra-material.

We come back to the 'break in the argument.' In what

[1] Thus, e.g., *ch'eng* appears in c. 12 and in c. 20. In the latter case, it is true, it appears only in the latter part of the chapter, namely after the point at which Professor Feng makes author B begin. But one of the chief difficulties I find in making the break at that point is that there is no obvious break at all in the argument or style until we come to c. 26.

sense a break and a change? First, Heaven and Earth are again considered in relation ostensibly to their dimensions, but leaving us doubtful whether a material heaven and earth are meant or not; a passage exuberant in style but confused in philosophic meaning and arriving at a different conclusion. It is not like our philosopher. Second, there follows a very emotional passage on the unique importance of ritual. From this the argument proceeds to the unique position of the Son of Heaven, who alone can decide on ritual and the rules and regulations which give the necessary uniformity to the life of the community. True kingship, however, must pass the test of whether it is true to the institutions of the sage-kings. Confucius saw all this, and he set forth the Way after the pattern of heaven and earth (? Heaven and Earth). He was . . . and there follows an extravagant list of his brilliant virtues. Finally—after the passage on civilization with its reintroduction of the idea of reality—the argument concludes with rather a medley of quotations from the *Book of Songs*, given to show that true government consists not so much in punishments as in the impalpable influence of virtue in the ruler: sentiments which remind us of third-century Taoism.

It is arguable that this point and the other in these chapters are compatible with our philosopher's position; and it is true that in the earlier chapters of *The Mean-in-action* a sense of the high importance of ritual and government by personality is shown, but not with this emotional flow which makes government by the Son of Heaven the supremely important thing in the world. Not only so: there is the reference to a standardization of weights and measures, of the width of carts for use on state roads, and of the forms of the ideographs. These were all measures which we know from reliable sources to have been put into effect by the First Emperor. And also, scattered throughout these chapters, there are all sorts of terms and phrases which are not found in books before the third century.[1]

[1] *Vide* Appendix III on suspiciously late terms in cc. 1, 26, second half, cc. 31, 33 to the end.

WHO WROTE THESE BOOKS? 99

The conclusion stares one in the face that here is a later addition to the original work.

There are, therefore, two great ideas in the book as a whole, and the second one burned in the mind of a man who had seen, or was actually seeing, all China unified under the rule of the First Emperor. Since unity and efficiency were good, he accepted the regime. But he was profoundly convinced that his Führer must, for his own sake as for the sake of the people, abandon his inhuman, totalitarian principles, and put the eternal verities of Confucius's teaching into practice. This was why he amplified the earlier book: he hoped to convert the emperor.

Thus, author A was a philosopher, concerned with the discovery of truth; author B was a high-minded theologian, concerned with politics. Two sections of the book being thus distinguished and the latter part being plainly datable as belonging to the second half of the third century B.C., when was the earlier part written?

The External Evidence in relation to Author A

To answer the above question we must consider the external evidence. That evidence, what there is of it, points to Tzu Ssu, Confucius's grandson and, therefore, at the height of his powers in the middle of the fifth century, more or less a contemporary of Mo Ti. First, there is the statement by Ssu-ma Ch'ien (145–86 B.C.), a genius of a historian (although not always reliable in details), who seems to have studied Confucius's family history on the spot. He says: 'Tzu Ssu was the author (*tso*) of the *Chung Yung*.' Alongside that, there is only the evidence in the catalogue of the Imperial Library towards the end of the first century B.C. There we find the title of a book, '*Tzu Ssu*, 23 *p'ien*' (divisions), in the section devoted to Confucianist non-canonical writings, and in the Canon Ritual section there is mention of a book called '*Chung Yung Shuo*, 2 *p'ien*,' without giving Tzu Ssu as author.[1]

[1] Professor Feng suggests that c. 1 is one *p'ien* of this book, and c. 20 (final section) to the end of the book is the other *p'ien*.

Then there is both the universal tradition that Tzu Ssu was the author, and reference in some Chou books to him as a figure in history.[1] Adding these stories together we get the impression of a quiet, retiring man who had no political ambitions, was learned in ritual, as his grandfather was before him, but not prepared to be more than a teacher of first principles: in a word, a rather philosophical kind of man. The only question is whether a thinker as early as Tsu Ssu was in the new age of reason is likely to have had the philosophical subtlety of mind that the A part of *The Mean-in-action* displays. The answer, of course, cannot be put as dogmatically as a plain 'Yes,' but there is this much to be advanced in support of the belief that a man of Tzu Ssu's time could reach this height. The *Analects* reveal a certain logical acuteness (*vide Analects*, VI, 23, and cp. V, 8) in Confucius's own mind. Mo Ti had his extraordinary gift of logic, and he was more or less of the same generation. Further, Chuang Chou, the brilliant Taoist writer of the fourth century B.C., shows a much more developed sense of the relativity of the material universe. What appears in *The Mean-in-action* as the idea in its plain, simple beginning is there carried to great lengths. Add to this the evidence in *Mencius*.[2]

In the light, therefore, of all the available evidence, internal and external, there seems no adequate reason for suspecting that Tzu Ssu was not author A, and a good deal of reason for believing that he was.

Who wrote 'The Great Learning'?

Examination of the language of *The Great Learning*, as shown above, produced a rather puzzling situation. On the one hand, it showed a certain simplicity of thought and language which we naturally take as a sign of an earlier date. On the other hand, there were signs which pointed

---

[1] Cp. Forke's *Geschichte der Alten Chinesische Philosophie* (Hamburg, 1927, pp. 158–68).
[2] *Vide* Appendix on Tzu Ssu in *Mencius* and the *T'an Kung*.

the other way. As a matter of fact, a number of phrases crop up in the text which are pretty clearly not early terms. Thus, to give three illustrations, there is strong reason for doubting whether the expressions *ch'i chi yü tzu* (lit. its pivot, i.e. the mechanics of the situation, is like this), and *chieh chü chih tao* (the way or principle of the measuring square) and *chung kuo* (middle kingdom, meaning the whole body of Chinese states) were used before the fourth century B.C. Further, the book shows an excellent command of the essay form of prose composition—practically every section starts with a statement of what it is about and ends with a statement that that is what has been explained—and we have every reason for believing that this literary form was not invented before Mo Ti had got into his stride as a teacher. It is safe, therefore, to assume that it was not till the fourth century was well started that thinkers generally were alive to the immense utility of this kind of writing. The Confucianists appear not to have taken kindly to it, but the disciples of Shang Yang, the Legalist, did. On this ground the presumption is that *The Great Learning*, being the style of book it is, could not have been produced before about the middle of the fourth century. This fits in with its quoting from the *Shu Ching* (*Book of Documents*). There is reason for supposing that this practice did not start before the fourth century.

In the light of the literary approach we are now in a position to look for the great idea in the author's mind, hoping thereby to find a clue to the problem of date. Since the stages in the argument are for the most part limpidly clear, there is no need, as in the case of *The Mean-in-action* to make an abstract. It is enough to read the introduction to the main body of the work, for there we find the great idea. It is contained in the words: 'From the Son of Heaven right down to the common people there is unity in this, that the bringing of the individual self into flower is of root importance.' The sentence has obviously been composed with immense attention to making it impressive. And then, almost immediately after—

according to the pre-Sung order—come the words: *tzu wei chih pen, tzu wei chih chih chih yeh* (this means knowing the root, this means the height of knowledge). I submit that what drove the author to write was his burning conviction that this flowering of moral personality was the basic thing in life, and that this flowering could not eventuate in a man unless he set himself to acquire knowledge and to keep on acquiring knowledge.

This is the first clue we get, and as a clue to the problem of date it does not take us very far. Any follower of Confucius might be expected to express such a conviction at any time from the fifth to the third century, and for that matter in any age since. We pass, therefore, to a study of the main body of the book, and here no passage seems to disclose a particular dominant purpose in the writer until we come to the last section. There we find: 'Win the people, and the country is won; lose the people, and the country is lost. . . . *Te* (power of moral personality) is the root, wealth is the branch.' These weighty sentences, together with the disproportionate length of this final section of the book, reveal a passion of denunciation against the position that wealth is the be-all and end-all of government.

I submit that this furnishes us with the clue we need to the date of the book's production. The author sets up *yi* (justice, ? righteousness) as the great means to national and international well-being. The book ends with 'profit is not to be taken as (real) profit; righteousness is to be taken as real profit.' Against that set the Legalist position in words attributed to Shang Yang (died 338 B.C.), the first pronounced Legalist with a philosophy of the State, 'What I call profit is the root of righteousness.' Compare also the two following sentences, the first from *The Great Learning*, the second from the *Shang Tzu*, the book embodying the tradition of Shang Yang's teaching: (1) 'In the *Odes* it is said: "Blessings on our lord, father and mother to his people. What the people like, he likes; what the people dislike, he dislikes."' (2) 'What the present age calls *yi* is the establishment of what people like and the abolition of what they dislike. . . . If the teaching given to the people is that of *yi*, then they will be lax, and if they are lax, then there will be anarchy.' Then let the student read over the two books and note the strongly controversial tone of both, the ethically-minded Confucianist on the one side, and the wholly materially-minded power worshipper on the other, and mark how the latter scorns knowledge and the flowering of personality. It is difficult to believe that the two books were not produced in the same age.

On the other hand, there is nothing in *The Great Learning* to show that the author has made up his mind against the distinctive philosophy of the Legalists. He does not use their word *fa* (a law) at all. Nor is there any indication that he knew of the catastrophic end to which Shang Yang came. If we want to make the two men more or less contemporaries, it is safer to assume that our author knew about Shang Yang in the day of his triumph when he had built up the resources of Ch'in State, and then, by an act of dastardly treachery defeated his own native land of Wei, and made Ch'in the dominant power in the Great Society. A suitable date would be some time between 350 and 340 B.C.

We reach this conclusion with the help of the great idea of the book, the distinctive Confucianist combination of growth of moral personality with the extension of learning, and the characteristic attack on the two-headed hydra that might is right and profit is right. Can we, with this clue, identify the author? That, alas, seems impossible. The only two traditional theories as to the authorship attribute it to Tzu Ssu or Tseng Ts'an. Owing to their early date, fifth century, both theories create difficulties, and when we examine the external evidence there is very little to be advanced in their favour. On the other hand, we can improve our acquaintance with our unknown author by one further step. As the study of the language shows, there is a simple, one might even say archaic, element in its style. Not only so, as prose it is highly distinctive for its pedagogic tone and the way the sentences lend themselves to repetition. Parts of the Mohist classic, the *Book of Mo Tzu*, have the same style, and, since we know from a later writer of excellent credibility, that the Mohist communities were in the habit of chanting their sacred book, we have corroborative evidence of the practice in the fourth century.

The question is, for what sort of pupils our good pedagogue made his text-book. The obvious answer is for young lordlings in some feudal court, for instance, Ch'i or Lu. There can be very little doubt but that they were taught, and, to judge by the exaggerated ideas Han writers had about late-Chou education, were taught in quite scholastic fashion. These young men were destined to hold high office in the State, one of them to be the head of it. In those days it was highly important that the country's leaders should be not only instructed in the code of chivalry, but also in the principles and practice of efficient government. On the other hand, these young men could hardly have taken to much intellectual discipline, or have been easily interested in scholars' questions. They had their hunting and shooting (archery) and the like to attract them. It was necessary to teach them with plain affirmations and vivid illustrations. Hence *The Great Learning*, a book which shows as no other classical book does the mind and technique of a born teacher.

TEXTS OF 'THE MEAN-IN-ACTION' AND 'THE GREAT LEARNING'

'THE MEAN-IN-ACTION'

The edition of *The Mean-in-action* on which the following translation is based is Juan Yüan's famous edition, *Sung Pen Shih Sang Ching Chu Shu Fu Chiao K'an Chi*. Since at certain points I have made sectional divisions which differ from those made by Chu Hsi, I have put his chapter numbers in parentheses. This, I trust, will be convenient for any English student reading Legge's edition of the text with translation and notes alongside this work.

SECTION I. An Appreciation of Tzu Ssu's *Mean-in-action* by a Later Scholar.

(c. 1.) That which Heaven entrusts to man is to be called his nature. The following out of this nature is to be called the Way. The cultivation of the Way is to be called instruction in systematic truth (*chiao*). The Way, it may not be abandoned for a moment. If it might be abandoned, it would not be the Way. Because this is so, the man of principle (*chun tzu*) holds himself restrained and keyed up in relation to the unseen world [lit. what he cannot see or hear]. Since there is nothing more manifest than what is hidden, nothing more visible than what is minute, therefore the man of principle is on guard when he is alone with himself.

¶ With the coming of the schools of thought came the idea of systems of truth. Thus the word *chiao* which in the *Analects* is only used as a verb, 'to instruct,' came by the third century B.C. to be used as a noun. An age of free thought leads to dogmatizing thinkers, and, after that, when the State recognizes one set of dogmas as the truth, its scholars tend to be dogmatic theologians. Confucianism became the established religion about a hundred years after this section was written.

The discovery of the individual to himself with new ranges of self-consciousness brought home to sensitive spirits the vital importance of interior honesty. Hence the emphasis among Confucianists and Taoists by the third century on a man in his solitude. Compare the early chapters of *The Great Learning*.

To have no emotions of pleasure and anger and sorrow and joy surging up, this is to be described as being in a state of equilibrium. To have these emotions surging up but all in tune, this is to be described as a state of harmony. This state of equilibrium is the supreme foundation, this state of harmony the highway, of the Great Society [? civilization]. Once equilibrium and harmony are achieved, heaven and earth maintain their proper positions, and all living things are nourished.

¶ Partly through their sense of the rhythm of the Four Seasons, partly through their cultivation of music, the Chinese early came to attach great importance to the idea of harmony. The political troubles of these late-Chou centuries and the cult of family religion strengthened the idea in them. Social harmony became one of their 'categorical imperatives,' an ideal which they have pursued with much the same difficulty which other peoples have experienced. But social harmony alone has never satisfied them. They have consistently cherished the aim of being in harmony with the great order of Nature, or that superhuman element in Nature which the authors of this book spoke of as Heaven.

SECTION II. Tzu Ssu invokes Confucius's Authority for the Idea of the Mean in Action.

(c. 2.) Chung-ni said: 'The man of true breeding is the mean in action.[1] The man of no breeding is the reverse. The relation of the man of true breeding to the mean in action is that, being a man of true breeding, he consistently holds to the Mean. The reverse relationship of the man of no breeding is that, being what he is, he has no sense of moral caution.'

(c. 3.) The Master said: 'Perfect is the mean in action, and for a long time now very few people have had the capacity for it.'

¶ To Confucius the times were out of joint. He thought of the age which Duke Chou inaugurated in much the same way as Catholics to-day think of the Middle Ages.

[1] Assuming that Confucius coined the phrase, it is better here to avoid printing it as a technical term. We may say that in Tzu Ssu's vocabulary it became a technical term.

(c. 4.) The Master said: 'I know why the Way is not pursued. (It is because) the learned run to excess and the ignorant fall short. I know why the Way is not understood. The good run to excess and the bad fall short. Amongst men there are none who do not eat and drink, but there are few who can really appreciate flavours.'

¶ The classical philosophers frequently illustrate a point by reference to the art of cooking. They were plainly very sensitive to the strength of man's appetite for food and drink, and they regarded the cook's art as a sign of civilization, highly capable of abuse, but also highly calculated to induce the refinement of temperance.

(c. 5.) The Master said: 'Alas, this failure to pursue the Way!

(c. 6.) The Master said: 'Consider Shun, the man of great wisdom. He loved to ask advice and to examine plain speech. He never referred to what was evil, and publicly praised what was good. By grasping these two extremes he put into effect the Mean among his people. In this way he was Shun [i.e. a sage-emperor], was he not?'

(c. 7.) The Master said: 'All men say "I know," but they are driven into nets, caughts in traps, fall into pitfalls, and not one knows how to avoid this. All man say "I know," but, should they choose the mean in action, they could not persist in it for a round month.'

(c. 8.) The Master said: 'Hui, a real man! He chose the mean in action, and, if he succeeded in one element of good, he grasped it firmly, cherished it in his bosom, and never let it go.'

¶ Hui was the one disciple who, Confucius felt, really understood and practised what he taught. He was deeply distressed over Hui's untimely death.

(c. 9.) The Master said: 'The states and families of the Great Society might have equal divisions (of land). Men might refuse noble station, and the wealth that goes with it. They might trample the naked sword under foot. But the mean in action, it is impossible for them to achieve that.'

¶ What precisely Confucius had in mind when he made this very discouraging statement, is very difficult to suggest. Obviously the mean in action must be a wonderful moral achievement if the admirable efforts described still fail to bring men to the required level. The next quotation, perhaps, throws some light on the matter, for the good pacifist and the good militarist are both included in the scope of the ideal. As will appear later, this ideal was to Tzu Ssu something wonderful, being both transcendent beyond ordinary moral ideas and, at the same time, inclusive of all conceivable moral situations. We can, therefore, understand his quoting the enigmatic saying.

(c. 10.) Tzu Lu inquired about strong men, and the Master said: 'Is it strong men of the southern kind (that you have in mind)? The strong man of the south is magnanimous and gentle in instructing people, and he takes no revenge for being treated vilely; it is the habit of a man of true breeding to be like this. The strong man of the north lives under arms and dies without a murmur: it is the habit of a man of true force to be like this. Hence the man of true breeding, how steadfast he is in his strength, having a spirit of concord and not giving way to pressure. He takes up a central position and does not waver one way or another. How steadfast his strength, for, when there is good government, he does not change his original principles, and, when there is vile government, he does not change, even though his life be at stake.'

(c. 11.) The Master said: 'To unravel mysteries and work miracles, that I will not do, even though my name should be recorded for ages to come. The man of true breeding follows the Way in all his acts, and it is impossible for me, therefore, to abandon the course half-way. The man of true breeding has faith in the mean in action. Although he live the life of a recluse, unknown to his age, he has no regrets. A man must be a sage to have this capacity.'

¶ I think it may be assumed that Confucius did not say this last sentence. Tzu Ssu might perhaps have added it, but it seems to me more like the third-century amplifier: cp. Sect. XVI, where this amplifier unconsciously reveals the extent to which idolization of Confucius had gone after two hundred years. In

Confucius's day, it would appear, men thought of King Wen and the like figures of antiquity as the *sheng wang*, the sage-kings—the Major Saints as we might call them—but they were prepared to concede a sort of second-class sage-hood to contemporaries who showed exceptional wisdom and benevolence. Even so, Confucius did not regard himself as being a really sage-like person.

The above quotations are all to the point. Also some of them are verifiable in the *Analects*, so that we can feel confident that Tsu Ssu was really inspired by his grandfather to think along these lines. The reader doubtless will feel that it is all very unsystematic; and I suspect that Tzu Ssu was aware that his teacher did not possess a systematic mind. But certain features of the mean in action have emerged. First of all, it is presented as a *tao*, a way, indeed, The Way, of men's well-being, the truth about life in a practical sense, although ordinary learning and goodness get it out of the true.

In the second place, it is not a summary of the highest martial virtue, nor of the highest pacific virtue. It must include both, presumably in some mysterious right proportion. But it is nothing to do with miracle-mongering or with the praise of men. Whatever It is, it is obviously of a transcendent nature. Having taken his reader thus far on the authority of his grandfather, Tzu Ssu now speaks in his own person, or rather in the text there comes a passage which is not preceded by 'The Master said.' Chu Hsi urged that this development of the argument came from Tzu Ssu, and clearly Chu Hsi was right.

SECTION III. The Material World is Limited, the Way Unlimited.

(c. 12.) The Way of the true man (*chun tzu*) is widely apparent and yet hidden.[1] Thus the ordinary man and woman, ignorant though they are, can yet have some knowledge of it; and yet in its perfection even a sage finds that there is something there which he does not know. Take the vast size of heaven-and-earth; men can still find room for criticism of it. Hence, when the enlightened man (*chun tzu*) speaks of supreme bigness, it cannot be contained within the world of our experience. Nor, when he speaks of supreme smallness, can it be split up in the world

[1] The Chinese word means normally 'to spend lavishly.' With no convincing emendation as a port of refuge, the translator can only do his best.

of our experience into nothing. As is said in the *Book of Songs*, 'The hawk beats its way up to the height of heaven, the fish dives down into the abyss.' That refers to things being examined from above and from below. Thus the Way of the man of principle: its early shoots coming into existence in the ordinary man and woman, but in its ultimate extent to be examined in the light of heaven-and-earth.

¶ In Chou religion the supreme overlord, the Son of Heaven, had in his capital an altar to Heaven and an altar to Earth: a lofty kind of animism. In the new age men came to think quite clearly of the visible heaven and solid earth as one vast order, the universe; but many of them still retained in their minds the idea of Heaven and of Earth, one or two omnipotent and benevolent Wills. This was intellectually confusing, of course; and it is confusing to us to-day as we read the classical literature, for we so often have to doubt what the writer meant, whether Heaven and Earth, or heaven and earth, or maybe Heaven-and-Earth, or heaven-and-earth. I doubt if Confucius was clear in his own mind, but I feel confident that Tzu Ssu was. When he thought of Will, he said Heaven. When he thought of the material universe, he said heaven-and-earth. His amplifier, on the other hand, was not clear. *Vide* Section XII.

We know from the *Book of Songs* that the order of the universe was criticized because men suffered. Following this idea of limitations to the universe, Tzu Ssu adapts it to his philosophic purposes. This heaven-and-earth, the biggest phenomenon of our experience, stops somewhere, but our idea of supreme bigness, as of supreme smallness, need not stop anywhere. The philosophically minded reader should compare this passage with Section XI. Tzu Ssu goes deeper there. Here he is content with making his point and drawing his moral, namely that one's view of anything, as, for instance, the material universe, depends on the angle from which you look at it. So with the Way of the Mean: it is both inexpressibly rare, and also part of the common stuff of life.

SECTION IV. Confucius's Authority invoked to show that the Way of the Mean is one which involves an Unlimited Demand on every sort of Individual, and also is mixed up with Religion.

(c. 13.) The Master said: 'The Way is not far removed from men. If a man pursues a way which removes him from men, he cannot be in The Way. In the *Book of Songs* there is the word, "When hewing an axe-handle, hew an axe-handle. The pattern of it is close at hand." You grasp an axe-handle to hew an axe-handle, although, when you look from the one to the other (i.e. from the pattern to the block of wood), they are very different. Therefore the right kind of ruler uses men to control men and attempts nothing beyond their correction; and fidelity and mutual service (these two human qualities) cannot be outside the scope of the Way. The treatment which you do not like for yourself you must not hand out to others. And this Way for the man of true breeding has four sides to it, in not one of which have I succeeded. To serve my father as I would have a son serve me as a father, in this I, Chiu,[1] have failed. To serve my prince as I would have a minister serve me as a prince, in this I, Chiu, have failed. To serve my elder brother as I would have a younger brother serve me as an elder brother, in this I, Chiu, have failed. To be beforehand in treating a friend as I would have him treat me as a friend, in this I, Chiu, have failed.'

¶ Most of this paragraph is not corroborated elsewhere as Confucius's own words; but Tzu Ssu has shown himself a reliable quoter, so it seems reasonable to assume that the statements made are from 'the Master.' Here, then, we see China's 'First of Teachers' taking his stand on that humanist foundation for which China has become so famous, not to say, in some circles of western thought, notorious. Man's Great Way of the Soul must be a human way, or perhaps Confucius would have preferred our word humane: a humane way. Not the least revealing of the statements here is Confucius's confession of personal failure. And in that connection it is important to note that Tzu Ssu, an ardent filial-pietist and therefore bound to protect his grandfather's reputation, had no compunction in quoting the confession. We may say that both men were too

---

[1] Chiu was another name Confucius had, and the one he would use in speaking of himself.

deeply concerned for man's spiritual welfare to have any thought for stained-glass attitudes.

The axe-handle may at first sight be a little puzzling, but really it is quite clear and forceful as an illustration. The ordinary run of men are the uncarved block and, to use the simile in *The Great Learning*, need to be carved and polished, to be cut and ground smooth in order that they may fulfil their high end. The pattern must be a human one. Presumably Confucius had Chou Kung and the other sage-kings in mind; but being a trained ritualist he might well be thinking also of the rituals, part religious part social in significance, which for him gave spiritual meaning to the humdrum affairs of daily life. With regard to the next paragraph, it is impossible to be sure, but it looks as if, with the exception of the last statement, it is Tzu Ssu speaking for himself. From this point on there is increasingly more of Tzu Ssu and less of Confucius.

(c. 14.) The acts of the true man agree with the station in life in which he finds himself, and he is not concerned with matters outside that station. If he is a man of wealth and high position, he acts as such. If he is a poor man and low in the social scale, he acts accordingly. So also, if he is among barbarians, or if he meets trouble. In fact, there is no situation into which he comes in which he is not himself. In a high station he does not disdain those beneath him. In a low station he does not cling round those above him. He puts himself in the right and seeks no favours. Thus he is free from ill will, having no resentment against either Heaven or men. He preserves an easy mind as he awaits the Will of Heaven: (in contrast to) the man who is not true, who walks in perilous paths and hopes for good luck. As the Master said: 'In archery there is a resemblance to the man of true breeding. If a man misses the target, he looks for the cause in himself.'

¶ Our philosopher is like the artists of later ages. He does not follow the pedestrian path of arguing from this to that about some abstract moral ideal. He waits till this feature and that of the true man rises clearly in his mind, and so makes a picture of him, leaving each line of his composition to make its own appeal.

(c..15.) The Way of the true man is like a long journey, since it must begin with the near at hand. It is like the ascent of a high mountain, since it must begin with the low ground. In the *Book of Songs* there is:

> The happy union with wife and child
>   Is like the music of lutes and harps.
> When concord grows between brother and brother,
>   The harmony is sweet and intimate.
> The ordering of your household,
>   Your joy in wife and child!

The Master said: 'How greatly parents are served in this!'

¶ As he paints his picture of the man of the Way, Tzu Ssu does not forget that he is engaged in setting forth an argument. Having dealt with the near, namely the common ways of life, he now proceeds to the distant, the numinous power in religious sacrifices. As he thought of this, he visualized the spiritual power of personality in the Great Dead. Again he quotes Confucius. Whether Confucius in what he said was referring to the manes of sage-kings—solemn sacrifices were made to such in different states—or to the manes of the various clans' High Ancestors, we cannot be sure. It is a point for the historians and hardly concerns the general reader.

(c. 16.) The Master said: 'How irrepressible is the spiritual power in the manes! Look for them and they are not to be seen. Listen for them, and they are not to be heard. They are in things, and there is nothing without them. They stir all the people in the Great Society to fast and purify themselves and wear their ritual robes, in order that they may sacrifice to them. They fill the air, as if above, as if on the left, as if on the right.[1] As the *Book of Songs* has it, 'The coming of the Spirits! Incalculable. And yet they cannot be disregarded.' Even so is the manifestation of the minute and the impossibility of hiding the real (*ch'eng*).

¶ The last sentence is surely Tzu Ssu's. I am tempted to translate *wei* not by the 'minute,' but by the 'invisible,' but I

---

[1] Cp. the *Record of Rites, Li Ch'i* (*Sacred Books of the East*, vol. xxvii, p. 412).

doubt whether Tzu Ssu regarded the Spirits as invisible in the sense in which we speak of 'things invisible' in contrast to 'things visible.' The old word 'subtile' about expresses the meaning of *wei*. This summing up by Tzu Ssu takes us back to his opening words in Section III where he inferred from the spatial limits of the sensible universe that there was something more and other than the material. It also prepares the way for the consideration later (*vide* Section VII et seq.) of this hidden core of reality in the universe, hidden, and yet impossible to hide.

I have had the experience of old scholars, devotees of the Chu Hsi intellectualization of the original Confucian teaching, shaking their heads dubiously to me over this passage. They doubted whether such a sympathetic appreciation of sacrificial religion was in Confucius's true vein. For my own part I do not doubt. He fought certain features in the religion current in his day, and so warned his disciples against spirit-mongering. He believed it was better to keep away from that sort of thing. But where religion seemed to him part and parcel of high ethical endeavour, he was in no sense opposed or indifferent to it. Thus he criticized certain phases of filial-piety religion on the ground of its low ethical standard; but, as will appear in the next section, he had a deep reverence for Shun, the Sage-King, who was famous for his exquisite filial piety.

SECTION V. Outstanding Personality cannot but have Wide and Continuing Influence, as is proved by the Hero-Saints of Tradition.

(c. 17.) The Master said: 'Consider Shun, the man of superb filial piety. By the virtue in him he was a sage. In his dignity he was Son of Heaven. In his wealth he owned all within the four seas. Temple sacrifices were made to him, and his memory was cherished by his descendants.[1] Thus it is that outstanding personality is bound to obtain its position of authority, its wealth, its fame, and its lasting life. For thus it is that Heaven, as it gives life to all creatures, can be surely trusted to give to each what

---

[1] Since these words of Confucius's do not occur elsewhere, it is impossible to be sure where the quotation ends.

is due to its basic capacity. And thus it is that the well-planted is nourished and the ill-planted falls prostrate.

The *Book of Songs* has the word:

> Hail to our sovereign prince!
> How gracious is his personality!
> He has put the people to right: he has put his men to right.
> Heaven has vouchsafed its bounty to him.
> Heaven has protected him and appointed him king;
> Heaven's blessing is his, not once but again and yet again.

Thus it is that the man of superb personality is bound to receive the commission from Heaven.

¶ The legend of Shun is one of the most touching in Chinese hagiography. He came of poor peasant stock. His father was blind and of a mulish disposition. His mother died when he was young, and his stepmother was a termagant, her son arrogant (*vide Yao Tien*). He spent himself in providing for them—when the field work was too much for him, the wild beasts came and helped him—and all he earned from his labours was the hatred of his family. In *Mencius* he is described as going out into the fields and crying aloud to pitying Heaven: 'What is it in me that makes my father and mother have no love for me?' The Sage-Emperor Yao, looking for a successor to the throne, chose him rather than appoint his own son or one of the great officers.

With regard to the 'commission from Heaven,' the Chou conquerors of the Yellow River area cultivated the idea that they had such a commission to destroy the Yin overlordship. Confucius firmly believed in this and helped to make the idea what it came to be, the central dogma of Confucianist political philosophy. That philosophy, so imbued with religious elements, saw a great pattern in history. Whenever a royal line became decadent and the people suffered from tyranny and incompetence, then that line lost its commission and Heaven appointed another man, one of outstanding *te*, to found a new line or Sons of Heaven. Tzu Ssu's mind moved in this direction.

(c. 18.) The Master said: 'The only man who has been without sorrow is King Wen.[1] He had Wang Chi for father and King Wu for son. The father laid the foundation, and the son built on it. King Wu thus inherited from

---

[1] For an example of the way in which the ritual revivalists in their times rhapsodized on King Wen, cp. *Record of Rites*, Bk. VI, Section 1.

a line of kingly men, T'ai Wang, Wang Chi, and King Wen. Once he had buckled on his armour, the world was his, for (although he rebelled) he suffered no loss to his world-wide reputation. In dignity he became the Son of Heaven, in wealth he owned all within the four seas. Temple sacrifices were made to him, and his memory was cherished by his descendants.'

It was in his old age that King Wu received the Commission, and it was Duke Chou who carried to completion the virtue in King Wen and King Wu. The rite reserved for sacrificing to a Son of Heaven he used for sacrificing to his (non-royal) forbears. And this rule in ritual was extended to the feudatories and great officers and was applied in every rank of society down to the minor officials and the common people. If the father was a great officer and the son a minor official, then the father was buried with the rite of a great officer, but afterwards was sacrificed to with the rite of a minor official. If the father was a minor official and the son a great officer, then the father was buried with the rite of a minor official, but afterwards was sacrificed to with the rite of a great officer. The practice of mourning for one year was extended to a great officer, of mourning for three years to a Son of Heaven. In the case of mourning for a father or a mother, there was no difference for the noble or the commoner. The practice was the same.

¶ Some readers may feel that all this is very remote. After all, we are not living in a feudal society—though Marxists affirm that we are—nor are we ancestor-worshippers. True, in our recently founded democracies the tendency is to be far less ancestor-conscious than the Chinese were two thousand years ago and are to-day. But Tzu Ssu's point here is not merely one for ancestor-worshippers. He was concerned with the question of continuity, continuity of individual personality in the continuing life of a society. His grandfather had impressed it on him that Duke Chou, the saintly statesman of old whose solemn memorial sacrifices the young Tzu Ssu probably had watched with awestruck eyes, was the hero to whom they all owed the great Chou order of society and the best institutions in their country of Lu. Personally I am reminded of the

Roosevelt-Willkie election and grandfathers impressing on their grandsons how the glorious Constitution of the United States goes back to Jefferson, and so to Washington. Jefferson looks to me a little like America's Duke Chou and Washington like King Wu who suffered no loss to his reputation in spite of leading a rebellion. I suppose that to ninety per cent of the religiously minded, the American Constitution, the constitution of American society, stands for something which helps them to believe in the continuity of their individual lives: their lives, and their children's lives. That is Tzu Ssu's point, except that we must realize that to him this power of spiritual continuity existed with high sacramental reality in the great personality. It is the great personality which carries on, is in men's blood and bones.

I hope my reader has marked the equalitarian strain in Tzu Ssu's thought. The culmination of this paragraph is that in Duke Chou's order of society, aristocratic though it was, when it came to children mourning for their parents, there were no distinctions of rank. The historian may well suspect that that was not a hundred per cent true of Tzu Ssu's society. But it was near enough to the truth to warrant Tzu Ssu's thinking of mourning for parents in the way he does.

(c. 19.) The Master said: 'How wide an influence King Wu's and Duke Chou's filial piety had.' Filial men are those who are well able to follow up what the men before have willed, and preserve what they have undertaken. In the spring and the autumn they repair their ancestral temples, arrange the sacrificial vessels, set in order the ceremonial robes, and offer the seasonal meats. The ritual of the temple is the means by which the line on the male side and the line on the female side are kept distinct. The gradation of titles is the means by which higher and lower ranks are defined. The distinctions of office are the means by which the worth of men is marked. In the pledging rite those of low station present the cup to those of high, and thus a place is made for the common man. At the festal board white-haired old men have their places, and by this means differences of age are observed. To maintain one's ancestors in their proper shrines, to carry out their rites, to play their music, to reverence those whom they honoured, to love those closely related to them, to serve the dead as they were served alive, to serve those who are no more as they were served when they were here: this is the height of filial piety. Let (a ruler) only grasp the significance of the rites at the altars of Heaven and Earth and those in the ancestral temple, and government will become (as easy) as pointing to the palm of the hand. For the rites to Heaven and Earth are means by which service is rendered to Shang Ti, the rites in the temple are the means by which (grateful) offerings are made to those from whom we have sprung.

¶ *Shang Ti* (lit. Above Ruler) appeared to the Protestant missionaries of the nineteenth century to approximate so nearly to the meaning of 'God' that it was adopted by most of them. The earlier Catholic missionaries used *T'ien Chu* (Heavenly Lord). In classical-era Confucianist works *Shang Ti* occurs fairly frequently, mainly in the *Book of Songs* and *Book of Documents* (*Shang Shu*), though nothing like so frequently as *T'ien* (Heaven). *Ti* goes back to the Yin era, being used then in reference to an earthly overlord. What the relation of *Shang Ti* to *T'ien* was in classical times, why, for example, the one term may be used in one sentence and the other in the next sentence, is one of the most difficult problems in Chinese studies. All I dare commit myself to here is that when using *Shang Ti* writers, on the whole, speak more anthropomorphically and anthropopathically than when using *T'ien*. I have a conjecture that in mid-Han times there was a movement in court circles towards theocracy,[1] and in this connection there was a revival of the old term *Shang Ti*—but that the movement failed. I surmise that the term had private-minded associations which set the best scholar thinkers against it.

SECTION VI. The Governing of Men.
(c. 20.) This section is a long one with various aspects of the subject clearly distinguished. I have, therefore, split it up into four subsections.
(1) The Primary Need for Men who can Govern.

[1] Cp. *Pai Hu Tung Yi* by Pan Ku, c. 1.

TEXT OF 'THE MEAN-IN-ACTION'

(par. 1.) The Duke Ai[1] asked advice as to governing, and the Master said: 'King Wen's and King Wu's system of government is revealed in the historical records. (par. 2.) It is this: with their kind of men the system worked: without their kind of men it came to an end. (par. 3.) Man's right way is to be prompt in good government as the earth's way is to be prompt in making things grow. Thus, good government is like the speed with which some reeds grow. (par. 4.) For this reason good government depends on the men (who govern). Such men are obtainable on the basis of their personality. The cultivation of personality is on the basis of the Way. The cultivation of the Way is on the basis of human-heartedness. (par. 5.) To be human-hearted is to be a man, and the chief element in human-heartedness is loving one's relations. So it is with justice: it is to put things right, and the chief element in it is employing worthy men in public service, whilst the degrees in kinship and the grades of office are the product of the established order of procedure. (par. 6.) (Unless those in the high ranks of society can capture the confidence of those in the lower ranks, they cannot gain the support of the people for their administrative measures.)[2] (par. 7.) Thus it is that the true ruler must not fail to cultivate his self; and, having it in mind to do this, he must not fail to serve his parents; and having it in mind to do this, he must not fail to have knowledge of men; and, having it in mind to have this knowledge, he must not fail to have knowledge of Heaven.

¶ Here is the famous Confucianist philosophy of government with its basic principle set forth: government must be by the personal example and influence of those who govern, and, if they are to achieve this, they must fit themselves accordingly.

---

[1] It was the Duke Ai who was responsible for Confucius, by then an old man, being recalled from his exile. To judge by several records, as they purport to be, it became in time a favourite practice to compare conversations between the Duke and the aged Sage. Cp. e.g. *Record of Rites* (*Sacred Books of the East*, vol. xxviii, pp. 255 et seq.) and the *Ta Tai Li Chi*.

[2] I accept Professor Feng's suggestion that this sentence, which is duplicated near the end of this section, is not required here.

This principle is sometimes criticized to-day, by Chinese thinkers as well as western, on the ground that it is too idealistic. The critics would seem to forget two things. One is that the theory was produced in that North China society at a time when it was suffering from stark individualism and unprincipled chauvinism, and that for a hundred and fifty years it was contested by powerful thinkers and men of action and, after that, its supporters were subjected to the scorn of the freebooting general who made himself the first Han Emperor. The theory managed to survive. The other thing is that, however much the world's bullies and fame-merchants and sensualists may dislike it, this may be the cold truth about man in society, and thus that there is no other way, as we might have been expected to learn from all the wars and other lesions in our bodies politic.

The phrase which I translated 'growing reeds' is Chu Hsi's interpretation of the text. The older commentaries did not emend the text. They agree with Ch'eng K'ang-ch'eng, whose explanation was that the author knew of a certain species of bee called *p'u lu* which took the mulberry caterpillar's young and fed it and so turned it into a *p'u lu*. This is rather an attractive interpretation, making government a matter of changing men; but in the light of the context and the emphasis on promptness, Chu Hsi's rendering is to be preferred.

(2) Those Aspects of Government which concern Everybody.

(par. 8.) There are five things which concern everybody in the Great Society, as also do the three means by which these five things are accomplished. To explain, the relationship between sovereign and subject, between father and son, between husband and wife, between elder and younger brother, and the equal intercourse of friend and friend, these five relationships concern everybody in the Great Society. Knowledge, human-heartedness, and fortitude, these three are the means; for these qualities are the spiritual power in society as a whole. The means by which this power is made effective is unity.

(par. 9.) Some people know these relationships by the light of nature. Others know them by learning about them from a teacher. Others, again, know them through hard experience. But once they all do know them, there is unity. Some people practise these relationships with a natural ease. Others derive worldly advantage from their practice of them. Others, again, have to force themselves to practise them. But once they all have achieved success in practising them, there is unity.

(par. 10.) The Master said: 'To love to learn is to be near to having knowledge. To put into practice vigorously is to be near to being human-hearted. To know the stings of shame is to be near to fortitude.[1] (par. 11.) So we may infer that the man who knows these three things, knows how to cultivate his self. When he knows how to do that, it may be inferred that he knows how to rule other individuals. And, when he knows how to do that, it may be inferred that he knows how to rule the whole of the Great Society with its states and families.

¶ This man, Tzu Ssu, is indeed a realist, in one part of his thinking, at any rate. Admitted that he assumes that man is an ethical being and that a society of men must embody some sort of particular moral power, or it has no unity to it, and that a society cannot embody this power unless most of its members have knowledge, human-heartedness, and fortitude. But he makes these assumptions on the basis that every man's life consists in relationships. He has just said that we must know men, i.e. know what they are, and so must know Heaven. These five relationships, therefore, are for him the given thing in man's life. They are the initial facts in the light of which ethical dispositions are seen to be means to ends. Does, for example, human-heartedness make a king more able to be king in relation to his subjects? Does it make the subjects each more able to be subjects in relation to their king? That is the test to be applied to human-heartedness as also to knowledge and fortitude. And this test is not merely in regard to that relationship, but also in regard to a man being a father to his son, and

---

[1] I proposed to my colleague, Mr. Wang Wei-ch'eng, that perhaps Confucius was referring to his own career here, to the time when he was an exile and his reputation was under serious suspicion. I suggested that the translation would be 'to experience loss of reputation is to be near to fortitude.' Mr. Wang was greatly shocked, and I was unable to understand on what grounds.

a son being a son to his father, and so on through the whole range of relationships, including the great equalitarian one between friend and friend. And then there is the patent realism in the way in which Tzu Ssu realizes how it takes all sorts to make a society, and how every man has a different lot, some being so placed that, for example, being a son is the most natural and easy thing for them, others being so placed that it is exactly the reverse. I suspect—one cannot do more, since Tzu Ssu is not explicit in the matter—that he realized the corollary to his position, namely that if the three means do not achieve the ends then there must be something wrong with a man's ideas about them. The king does not give up trying to be king and a subject, etc.—he cannot do that because that means giving up living —but he has to set himself to know better what knowledge, human-heartedness, and fortitude are.

May I suggest that a good deal of our western ethical thinking has been vitiated by a tendency to be too idealistic, by men thinking in terms of moral ideals rather than in terms of fundamental given relationships? The penalty for doing that is that either a man goes on without putting his ideals into practice, just waiting for an ideal state of affairs, or he tries to make all life square with his ideas about justice and love or whatever may be the abstractions to which he blindly pins his faith. Whilst, therefore, we may criticize Tzu Ssu's list of five relationships and three means as incomplete—different cultures with their differing Great Traditions may be expected to throw varied lights on these matters—we cannot criticize his insistence on facts being faced first and ideals being tested by concrete reality.

Nor can we criticize Tzu Ssu's assumption about unity in society. A nation is not a nation unless there is, to use Rousseau's expression, a general will, and how a society is to get that apart from the ordinary relationships of man and man passes comprehension. But, of course, unity is not uniformity. How could it be with every one's circumstances different from every one else's? So, if Tzu Ssu had been alive to-day, he would surely have opposed the Nazi idea of a regimented uniformity. In fact, we can see in Tzu Ssu's words here an answer to the theory of political uniformity which Mo Ti was preaching in his day, and which led on to the totalitarian theories of the Legalists.

(3) The Basic Duties of Rulers.

(par. 12.) For those whose function covers the whole

Great Society or any one of its constituent states, there are nine basic duties: cultivation of one's self, honouring men of worth, affectionate treatment of the royal family, high respect towards ministers of state, courtesy towards all the other officers, fatherly care of the common people, promotion of the hundred crafts, kindly treatment of strangers, enlistment of the fervent loyalty of the fief-holders. (par. 13.) Let the self be cultivated, then the Way is established in the country. Let the right men be put into the right posts, then mistakes [? in administration] will not occur. Let the royal family be treated affectionately, then the royal uncles and cousins will bear no ill will. Let the ministers of state be held in high respect, then there will be no vacillation in policy. Let courtesy be extended to all the other officers, then the lower ranks will doubly repay that courtesy. Let fatherly care be bestowed on the common people, then they will gladly obey. Let the hundred crafts be promoted, then the resources for expenditure will be ample. Let strangers be treated with kindness, then men from all parts will be attracted. Let the loyalty of the fief-holders be enlisted, then the whole Great Society will stand in awe of the Throne.

¶ This passage gives us a little insight into the various problems with which the overlord of this feudal society, or the rulers of states who were on the way to become kings, had to deal. I think we must assume that since the cultivation of the self is put first on the list, Tzu Ssu states the problems in order of relative importance; but there is no need to press this, particularly as the problem of the fief-holders—one would have thought a very thorny one—is put last in the series. Perhaps, however, Tzu Ssu did this knowing he was being paradoxical, but wishing to show that the more important business was to get everybody else living happily, since then the fief-holders would get no support for any plots to rebel. We know enough of the Great Society and its constituent states at that time to understand a wise man thinking that nothing could stop ambitious fief-holders from plotting, and the only thing to do was to prevent their getting any public support. The special reference to the royal family is intriguing to our western minds. There the point to note is that the successor to the throne or to a dukedom was not by any means necessarily the eldest son, and there were endless intrigues in the palace courts over this son or the other being made heir apparent. Filial piety came into this matter, for the new king or duke was bound by religion to remember that his brothers and uncles and cousins were of the same blood as his sacred parents and grandparents.

(par. 14.) (At the times of solemn sacrifice) when purification is to be made and ritual robes to be worn, if nothing be done in contravention of the established order of procedure (*li*), this is the means by which the individual self is cultivated. If intriguers be expelled from court and seductive beauties kept well away, if riches be regarded lightly and the virtue in men be prized, men of worth are thereby encouraged. If high titles together with generous allowances be given to the members of the royal family, if sympathy be shown with their natural likes and dislikes, they are thereby encouraged to family affection. If their departments be enlarged, and they be given full responsibility, ministers of state are thereby encouraged. If an honest confidence be given to them and allowances be on a generous scale, lower ranks of officers are thereby encouraged. If the corvée be used only at the farmer's slack time and the taxes be lightened, the common people are thereby encouraged. If daily and monthly trials of skill be held, and grants of better rations be given on the merit of the work done, the hundred crafts are thereby encouraged. If they be escorted on their return and welcomed on their arrival, if those who are men of merit be entertained and those who are not be given charity, kindness is thereby shown to strangers. If arrangements be made for sacrifices in great families whose line of succession has been broken, and fiefs which have been extinguished be restored, if order be made where anarchy prevails and support be given where there is danger from attack, and if courts be held at stated intervals and a generous bounty be dispensed at their close with a moderate tribute required at their opening, the fervent loyalty of the fief-holders is thereby enlisted. (par. 15.) These are the nine basic duties for the men whose function covers the whole Great Society or one of its states. By the practice of these duties and the way in which they work, there is unity.

¶ This passage strikes me as dubious. For one thing, the previous passage has about expressed all that seemed required on these basic duties. For another, I do not quite see Tzu Ssu, the philosopher, deeply religious though he was and ritualist at that, taking up so exaggerated a position as the one revealed in the first sentence. For a third, the reference to restoring sacrifices in great families whose lines have been extinguished arouses the historian's suspicions. Not that fiefs had not been getting extinguished, as we saw in Chapter III of the Introduction, and it may be that the reference here is to the sacrifices to the old Yin and Hsia kings which were kept up in Chou times. But the *kuo* (states) hardly bears out that interpretation. It is possible that the religious side to Tzu Ssu gave him the idea that a pious prince would show most admirable virtue by restoring such sacrifices. On the other hand, I do not know of an actual case of a prince doing this until the Han Dynasty time, when in 134 B.C. Wu Ti restored the ancestral houses in seven *kuo* (vide *Ch'ien Han Shu*, chüan 6). The passage need not, therefore, be taken as coming from Tzu Ssu. It is possible it comes from his amplifier in the third century B.C., for that first sentence is quite in his vein. Also it is possible that a very idealistic ritualist of the First Emperor's time may have thought of him as doing this pious and placatory act.

(4) The Necessity for Unremitting Effort and for Truth and Reality in the Self.

(par. 16.) In the transaction of business success depends on preparation beforehand: without preparation there will be failure. If you decide beforehand what you are going to say, (when the time comes, you will not stutter and stammer; and if you are decided on what you are setting out to do, you will fall into no quandaries. Decide (therefore) beforehand what conduct should be, and then there will be no regrets: decide beforehand what the Way is, and then there will be no limit to the result [? spiritual results]. (par. 17.) Thus, unless those in the higher ranks of society can capture the confidence of those in the lower ranks it is impossible for them to gain the support of the people for their administrative measures. But there is only one way by which this confidence may be captured; for, if friends cannot trust each other, there can be no confidence in the men in the higher ranks. But there is only one way by which friends can come to trust each other; for, if men are not dutiful to their parents, there can be no trust between them as friends. But there is only one way for men to be dutiful to their parents; for, if in rounding in on themselves, they are not true, they cannot be dutiful to their parents. But there is only one way for a man to have a true and real self; for, if he does not understand the good, he cannot be true and real in himself.

¶ At one or two points in this Section VI there have been signs of a pedagogic mind speaking. In this last subsection it is very apparent. The reader will remember that Tzu Ssu is recorded as having become in his later years mentor to the Duke of Lu. He would appear to have thought out the business side of administration with some care.

The final sentences are the turning point of the argument of the book as a whole. The metaphysical quality of reality—or realness, as the reader must be prepared to find it called from time to time in this translation—now absorbs the attention of the author. The term *chung-yung* (the mean in action) has not figured in the argument since early in the book, and that is a fact which the critic must take into account. But *Tao* (the Way), which from the beginning has been a synonym for the *chung-yung*, has been constantly in use. In this second and main stage in the argument the aim of the author would appear to have been to prove that although man is irrevocably wrapped up in the society of men, including the great company of the dead, yet all the phenomena of life lead us to visualize one supreme phenomenon, individual personality. Not self-centred individuality: whatever may not be clear in the argument, that at least is clear; but a person, a man, a woman, as Heaven means them to be— though we may doubt whether it ever occurred to the author that a woman might be a sage. Having proved this fact and with it the unity of life, he now launches out into a philosophical inquiry. It is rightly described as philosophical, because he is concerned with establishing the reality which underlies this fact of individual personality. But those who are called realists in the society of western moral philosophers may be tempted to regard Tzu Ssu as a pure mystic. If they do, it will be curious, since he has shown himself fully awake to those everyday relationships, not to speak of the seamy side of court life, and the hard lot of the peasants, to which the modern realists rightly insist due attention must be paid. Whether the author is a poet-mystic rather than a philosopher is a question to which the reader's own judgment must lead him to find his own answer.

SECTION VII. Reality in Heaven and Realness in Man.
(c. 20, par. 18.) It is the characteristic of Heaven to BE the real. It is the characteristic of man to be coming-to-be-real. (For a man) to be real [i.e. to have achieved realness] is to hit the Mean without effort, to have it without thinking of it, entirely naturally to be centred in the Way. This is to be a sage. To be coming-to-be-real is to choose the good and to hold fast to it. This involves learning all about the good, asking about it, thinking it over carefully, getting it clear by contrast, and faithfully putting it into practice. If there is any part about which he has not learnt or asked questions, which he has not thought over and got clear by contrast, or which he has not put into practice, he sets to work to learn and ask and think and get clear and put into practice. If he does not get the required result, he still does not give up working. When he sees other men succeeding by one effort, or it may be a hundred, he is prepared to add a hundredfold to his own efforts. The man who can last this course, although he is stupid, will come to understand: although he is weak, will become strong.

(c. 21.) To (be able to) proceed from (the capacity for) realness to understanding is to be ascribed to the nature of man. To proceed from understanding to realness is to be ascribed to instruction in truth. Logically, realness involves understanding and understanding involves realness.

¶ The philosophical reader may well want to know whether my distinction between Reality and Realness is borne out by the Chinese in any way. As far as actual words go it is not. The same character is used in relation to both Heaven and man. But our author makes so clear a distinction between Heaven and man in this connection and stresses that a man normally is only on the way to achieve the reality of Heaven, that his human counterpart to what is perfect in Heaven seems better expressed by a slightly different term. The idea came to me when reading Leibniz, whom, as the reader knows, I regard as having a fundamentally similar metaphysic to Tzu Ssu's (cp. Introduction, Chapter I).

There would appear to be a lapse in the logic of the last paragraph. If it is man's nature to proceed from realness, or rather a capacity for realness, to understanding, then there are no circumstances in which instruction is needed. Actually, to judge by the book as a whole, Tzu Ssu's position clearly is that what a man has by nature does not necessarily come to fruition, or 'completion,' as he would say. Hence, there is an implicit assumption that if a man does not proceed to understanding, the capacity for realness in him will inevitably be affected. To avoid this happening there is scope for *chiao* (instruction, education).

SECTION VIII. Human Realness in Action: its Power to bring Completion in Development.

(c. 22.) It is only the man who is entirely real in this world of experience who has the power to give full development to his own nature. If he has that power, it follows that he has the power to give full development to other men's nature. If he has that power, it follows that he has the power to give full development to the natures of the creatures. Thus it is possible for him to be assisting the transforming, nourishing work of heaven and earth. That being so, it is possible for him to be part of a trinity of power (heaven, earth, and himself).

(c. 23.) For, in the second place, with regard to the lop-sided man, he can have realness. Assuming there is realness, the inference is that it takes on form. If it takes on form, then it is conspicuous. If conspicuous, then full of light: if full of light, then stirring things: if stirring things, then changing them: if changing them, then transforming them. Thus it is only the man who is entirely real in the world of experience who has the capacity to transform.

¶ First, the opening words of the paragraph are very difficult in the Chinese.[1] I have taken the liberty, as I did in Section III, of translating *t'ien hsia* as 'world of experience,' by which I mean sensible experience. There are to me clear signs in *The Mean-in-action* of Tzu Ssu wanting to express thoughts for which the language he had at his command was hardly adequate. This applies also to *chih* (entirely) which I am tempted to translate by 'unadulterately.' If Tzu Ssu was not a fantastic idealist his *chih ch'eng* (entirely real) does not refer to a perfect embodiment of Heaven's reality in man, but to a relative amount of realness in him, relative but unadulterated, unvitiated by the opposites to knowledge and human-heartedness and courage. It is, I would urge, significant that he does not mention the sage here.

Second, what did the man who wrote these words think about man's nature? Did he regard it as having a natural aptitude for goodness or the reverse? The question may not have become a sharp issue in his mind as it became, for example, in Mencius's mind, or in the West for Pelagius and St. Augustine. There is no sign that Confucius applied his mind to the issue, nor is there any sign in this book that Tzu Ssu did. But he did realize the simple fact of human growth and development, the child becoming the man, and the development of man's civilization. His grandfather taught him to see these things. On the top of this he was convinced of Heaven's Reality and man's capacity for something essentially the same. This, he infers, is the secret of true development. And since one man's world of sensible experience is the same as everybody else's, the man who has the capacity of realness is thereby able to reinforce to the fullest extent the same capacity in other people. Further, since the world in which the seasons change and things grow is the same world as the world of men, Tzu Ssu infers that if any man anywhere has an effectual power of realness in him, it must act as a reinforcement to the fullest extent of the powers of development in Nature, where everything has its own natural capacity waiting to be developed.

Third, a great many people have objected and do object to the linking of man with the order of Nature in this fashion. At

---

[1] Cp. *Hsun Tzu*, chüan 15, p. 5.

the one extreme Legge, a representative of nineteenth-century Protestantism, took heaven and earth to be Heaven and Earth, and in his comment on this passage (*vide Chinese Classics*, 1893, vol i., p. 416) exclaimed: 'What is it but extravagance thus to file man with the Supreme Power.' At the other extreme, thorough-going materialistic rationalists would deny that there is any such spiritual reality in man, and therefore, although man can assist the nourishing powers of Nature, it is only because he is part of Nature, on the same footing as animals and plants, driven by the same mechanical compulsions which operate in their seasonal flourishing and decay. Mr. Bertrand Russell, I take it, would say that we can make no assumptions either way; but it would be very interesting to know what his *ad hoc* reply would be to the various provocations of this paragraph. Leibniz, it is to be hoped, has met Tzu Ssu and Chu Hsi on the other side, and the three thinkers have come to an amicable agreement, perhaps having St. Paul into the discussion with his 'earnest expectation of the creature waiteth for the manifestations of the sons of God.

I have some doubts about the end of the passage, from 'For, in the second place' onwards. It looks a little like the Amplifier, who, as we shall see in Section XII, was not always clear in his mind whether he was talking literally or metaphorically. However, I have translated as if the words were Tzu Ssu's.

SECTION IX. Human Realness in Action: the Ability to Foreknow.

(c. 24.) A characteristic of the entirely real man is that he is able to foreknow. When a country is about to flourish, there are bound to be omens of good. When it is about to perish, there are bound to be omens of evil fortune. These are revealed in the milfoil and (the lines on the shell of) the tortoise. They affect the four limbs. When disasters or blessings are on the way, the morally good and the morally evil (elements) in a country are bound to be known first of all. Thus the entirely real man has a likeness to the divine.

¶ *Shen* (the divine) might perhaps be translated by 'superhuman,' but we should be no nearer the meaning. Tzu Ssu believed in spirits (cp. Section IV), but does not explain where he places them exactly in relation to Heaven or to man.

The reader who is ignorant of Chinese thought should not be too surprised at the reference to divination. He would do well to recall such beliefs as are represented by Eryximachus's statement in Plato's *Symposium*: 'All sacrifices and the whole province of divination which is the art of communion between gods and men—these, I say, are concerned only with the good and the cure of the evil love.' Just before he had said: 'the wanton love, getting the upper hand and affecting the seasons of the year, is very injurious and destructive, and is the source of pestilence.' (Jowett.) The awakening of the mind to its power of self-conscious reasoning does not necessarily destroy beliefs in a moral order of the universe. Very often, as was the case with Tzu Ssu's age in China, the new powers of the mind are extensively used to buttress faith in this order. Thus the discovery of a wide range to the operation of cause and effect may produce, at any rate for the time being, an enhanced belief in divination.

SECTION X. Realness again in relation to Completion of Things.

(c. 25.) Realness is self-completing, and the way of it is to be self-directing. Realness is the end as well as the beginning of things, for without realness there would be no things at all: which is the reason why the true man prizes above everything coming-to-be-real. Realness is not merely a matter of an individual completing himself. It is also that by which things in general are completed. The completing of the individual self involves man-to-man-ness (*jen*). The completing of things in general involves knowledge. Man-to-man-ness and knowledge are spiritual powers (*te*) inherent in man, and they are the bridge [lit. *tao*, way] bringing together the outer and the inner. Hence it is self-evidently right that realness should function continuously.

¶ It is tempting to comment on this, but I have already allowed myself overmuch latitude in this second main stage of Tzu Ssu's argument. If the reader cannot weigh up for himself the affirmations here made, any comments of mine would be of little use to him. There is, however, one exception, the cryptic remark about bringing together the outer and the inner. I take this to denote the not-self (outer) and the self (inner). That is more likely than the alternative interpretation of the material world and the spiritual, for there was no dichotomy between these two worlds in Tzu Ssu's mind. Also, realness itself would surely be for him the obvious bridge linking the material and the spiritual. Since *jen* is one of the strands of his bridge of harmony between the not-self and the self, I have translated it here by man-to-man-ness instead of human-heartedness: for the completion of the individual self is not achieved by mere fellow-feeling between man and man but by feelings and aspiration plus action. Quite how Tzu Ssu regarded knowledge as making for the completion of beings outside oneself is not very clear; but perhaps he had some inkling of what knowledge (*scientia*) to-day has done in relation to the world of Nature.

SECTION XI. Realness transcends the Material.

(c. 26.) The result is that entire realness never ceases for a moment. Now if that be so, then it must be extended in time: if extended in time, then capable of proof: if capable of proof, then extended in space-length: if extended in length, then extended in area: if extended in area, then extended in height-visibility.[1] And this quality of extension in area is what makes material things supportable from below: this quality of extension in height-visibility is what makes things coverable from above: whilst the extension in time is what makes them capable of completion. Thus area pairs with earth, height-visibility with heaven, and space plus time makes limitlessness. This being its nature, it is not visible and yet clearly visible, does not (deliberately) stir things and yet changes them, takes no action and yet completes them.

¶ A very impressive, though in some respects very curious, chain of inferences relating realness to time and space. It is, of course, of great interest to find so early a thinker getting down to the three dimensions of space. 'Capable of proof' presumably refers to proof on the evidence of the senses. We can see how, having these in mind, Tzu Ssu can make his next link in

---

[1] I take *kao-ming* as Tzu Ssu's attempt, with the language at his disposal, to express the third dimension. Cp. *Han Fei*, c. 20.

the chain and get from time into space. But the important part of the argument is the final conclusion which takes him beyond the limited sensible universe into 'limitlessness,' which in this context might almost be translated by 'infinity-eternity.' I confess I do not see exactly how the combination of space and time could have suggested this conclusion to our philosopher, unless the idea of 'matching earth' and 'matching heaven' called up in his mind the idea of a spirit-Earth and a spirit-Heaven. In the language of sacrifices to ancestors a particularly exalted personality such as King Wen was said to *pe'i* (pair with) Heaven. If that happened Tzu Ssu slipped up in his logic. Tzu Ssu was not the only early thinker who had a philosophic idea of a space-time universe lying, so to speak, next door to a spiritual one. In Chuang Chou, the Taoist genius, a hundred and fifty years later, the idea crops up again, e.g. in his imaginative story of Lieh Tzu: he could ride on the wind with the precision of his skill, being away for fifteen days before returning. Rarely does a man attain the happiness he had. And yet, although he was free from the necessity of walking, there was still something he depended on. But suppose he had been borne on the 'eternal fitness of Heaven and Earth, driving before him the elements as his team while roaming through the realms of For-ever, upon what then would he have had to depend?'[1] I would suggest to students that Chuang Chou in this chapter shows more than one trace of Tzu Ssu's influence.[2] The 'takes no action . . .' will surprise readers who have heard of the Taoist *wu-wei* (inaction). Cp. Appendix on *Wu-wei*.

SECTION XII. The Amplifier Illustrating the Previous Argument in his own Way.

(*Author B (cp. Introduction, Chapter IV) here begins his part of the book.*)

The Way of Heaven-and-Earth may be summed up in a word, namely, their function in relation to all things is unique, and consequently their giving of life to all things is unfathomable. The Way of Heaven-and-Earth is large, is substantial, is high, is brilliant, is far-reaching, is long-enduring. But take now the heaven before us with its

---

[1] The words within inverted commas are from Giles's *Chuang Tzu* (Shanghai, 1926), p. 5.
[2] Cp. also *Huai Nan Hung Lieh*, c. 1, *init*.

bits of brightness: and yet viewed in its inexhaustible extent with its network of sun and moon and stars, constituting the canopy over all creation. Let us take this earth before us, a handful of soil: and yet bearing the burden of the Hua Mountains and the rivers and the seas without feeling the weight or letting the water seep away. Take this mountain, just a fistful of stones: and yet on its broad flanks producing plants and trees, making a home for birds and beasts, and storing within masses of precious stones and metals. Take this piece of water, just a ladleful:[1] and yet in its plumbless depths producing all the fishes and monsters of the deep which are of so great profit to mankind. The *Book of Songs* has the words: 'Heaven's decrees, how gloriously unceasing they are': which means that this is what makes heaven to be Heaven. And again, 'How concealed from view was the purity of spiritual power (*te*) in King Wen': which means that this was what made King Wen to be *wen*[2] (the civilizer): for purity does not stop.

The words 'large,' 'substantial,' etc., are the same Chinese words as translated in the previous section by 'area,' etc. Students of Legge's translation will note that 'large,' etc., are his words both here and in the previous section. Legge thought that the two passages came from the same hand. Also he took it for granted, apparently, that the author was using these spatial terms in a metaphorical sense. My contention is that Tzu Ssu used them literally, and only the Amplifier used them in a blurred, half-literal, half-metaphorical way.

This Amplifier obviously is not to be despised as a writer. He has a power of vivid language, is indeed something of a poet. Unfortunately—for the critic, fortunately—he misunderstood Tzu Ssu's position, for he speaks of the material heaven and earth as inexhaustible in extent. That is precisely what Tzu Ssu took it not to be.

---

[1] Presumably refers to the China Sea. Of the monsters of the deep specified in the text I have been unable to track down reliable names for three. For this reason I do not specify.

[2] The two characters are the same.

SECTION XIII. The Amplifier exalts the Ritual Code.

(c. 27.) How supreme is the Way of the sage man, (the influence of it) spreading far and wide like the ocean. His Way nourishes all creation. Its influence reaches to the height of heaven. And how yet more supreme are the Three Hundred Maxims of the Ritual Code, and the ten times more on discipline in conduct. 'Unless the power of personality (*te*) be of the highest, the highest result of the Way cannot be consolidated.' Therefore the enlightened man does homage to the spiritual power (*te*) which is his by nature and applies himself to personal study (of *li*). The further afield he goes in this, the more he explores the hidden subtleties. At the peak of enlightenment the mean in action directs him. Thus it is that he studies the old past and comes to know the new present, and gives earnest attention to (the principles and practice of) the Ritual Code.

It follows from this that in a high position the enlightened man is not proud, in a low position he is not insubordinate. When things are right in the country his advice is such that he has to be employed. When things are wrong, his silence is such that he cannot be treated harshly. Is not this the meaning of the saying in the *Book of Songs*: (c. 28.) 'His intelligence and wisdom are a protection to himself'? As the Master said: 'To be ignorant and have a passion for one's own opinion, to be in a low position and be entirely self-willed, to live in the world to-day and go continually back to the old ways: people of this sort invite calamity on themselves.'

¶ This exaltation of ritual will leave Christians of the Protestant tradition cold. May I, as a man glad to have been trained in this tradition but seeing certain grave spiritual deficiencies in it, suggest that along with the cult of ritual goes the profound and fruitful idea that the life of man is illumined by truth and reality breaking out as light at certain specific points. In other words, without the sacramental in our life, it is either brutish or coldly rational.

The last paragraph had a poignant interest. The Amplifier

would appear to be nervous whether his opinions may cause umbrage and suspicion in high quarters.

SECTION XIV. The Son of Heaven's Unique Responsibility.

(c. 28, par. 2.) The Son of Heaven is the only person who has the right to decide the rules of *li* (ritual), the weights and measures, and the forms of the characters. Take the Great Society as we see it to-day. Carriage wheels have to be a uniform distance apart, books have to be written in uniform characters, and conduct is regulated by uniform relationships. Although a man occupy the throne, if he has not the corresponding moral personality, he has not the right to make new rituals and music. Nor if he has the moral personality but does not occupy the throne has he this right. The Master said: 'I can speak of the Hsia Ritual, but (the authorities in) Chih State cannot prove what they were. I can study the Yin Ritual, because it still exists in Sung State. Actually I study the Chou Ritual, for it is in use to-day. I follow Chou.'

¶ This statement of Confucius's was apparently much prized by the Ju in the ages after him. The point of its introduction here is that Confucius did not occupy the throne, and therefore could not dare to change the established institutions and their rituals. But he was a sage, and, therefore, the new regime could not go wrong if it followed his example.

The systematization of life in the Great Society as described here by four striking examples was the work of the First Emperor. Before he came to supreme power no one, certainly no shadow king in the Chou capital, was in a position to stop the schismatic tendencies in the Great Society. Civilization was on the way, but a very materialistic and 'smart-Aleck' one. It is increasingly clear that local variations in the common script were becoming more numerous, so that new languages were on the way, as they came in Italy, France, and Spain after the destruction of Roman authority. The First Emperor had hacked his way to the throne and destroyed the time-hallowed landmarks, e.g. the old state divisions were abolished. But by his insistence on uniformity he opened the way for something better. The Han regime, which created the great cultural and political union on the geographical scale which we associate with the word 'China,' owed a great deal to the regime which it superseded and the tyrant whom its rulers execrated.

For those who to-day are joined in an implacable opposition to the Nazi plans for unifying Europe, this almost determinative phase in Chinese history arouses a sobering train of thought. The rise of the modern states in Europe on the ruins of feudalism seemed so good a thing to our fathers. They believed so honestly that in spite of its weaknesses our civilization was civilization; and a noble American philosopher of two generations back taught men widely to think of the 'Great Society.' Yet the schisms in our midst, political, economic, and cultural, now show themselves as such poisonous growths that only the staunchest of idealists dare think of the Great Society of the future. Have we got to go through a totalitarian furnace, if not this time, then next, before we learn our Way of the Mean?

SECTION XV. The Only Way in which a Monarch can obtain Obedience.

(c. 29.) If the man who exercises kingship in the Great Society has the three important matters (of ritual, weights and measures, and the forms of the characters) in hand, he will seldom go wrong. But, if the man at the head be good but does not give such visible proof of his goodness, then, being unattested, he does not inspire confidence, and the people, in consequence, do not obey. So also with his officials if they be good but have no respect (for the regulations which they enforce): they also do not inspire confidence, and the people, in consequence, do not obey. Thus it is that the Way of the true monarch is rooted and grounded in his own personality and proves itself in the eyes of the people, bears examination by the Three Sage-Kings, and reveals no fundamental errors: is built up in accord with Heaven-and-Earth and shows no contradiction (of its laws): is tested in relation to the manes and creates no doubts: and is able without society going astray to wait a hundred generations for a sage. If (a monarch's way) can stand the test in relation to the manes, then he has understanding of Heaven. If it can thus wait a hundred generations for a sage man without leading society astray, then he has understanding of man. And thus it is that the true monarch's influence may last for generations as the Way for the Great Society, and his deeds be an example and his words a pattern. Then people in far-off places will look longingly to him; and those who are near will not grow weary of him. The *Book of Songs* has the words: 'In this quarter no hatred (of him), in that no wearying. Almost without ceasing night and day they continue their praises.' There never has been a true monarch of this kind who became widely known as 'a highly reputable parasite.'

¶ In this last sentence I have ventured to emend the text, omitting *pu* (not) before 'of this kind.' The commentators have had immense trouble with the text as it stands, for the reason that *tsao yu yü* (a flea having a reputation) apparently defied explanation. Thus the practice has been to emend the character for 'flea' to the character for 'early' which has the same sound, *tsao*. But for so brilliant a stylist as the Amplifier to end a highly impressive argument with 'There never has been a true monarch not like this who early had a reputation in the Great Society' is surely very difficult to believe. *Tsao yu yü* on the face of it is a proverbial saying, and fortunately there is in *Mencius* the story from which the saying came into existence. A certain decayed gentleman of Ch'i State living in the capital daily went out and on returning in the evening scorned the simple food prepared by his wife. He loftily told her that he had been dining with the best people. Since her 'goodman' never brought any guests home, the wife's curiosity was aroused. She followed him one morning and discovered to her horror and disgust that he went outside the city to where the graves of the best families were and begged food from those sacrificing to the dead. I submit that this incident became widely known and 'a highly reputable parasite' became the derisive term for a man in a high position who battened on society. The Chinese have a gift for sarcasm to-day, and those who are familiar with *Chuang Tzu* and the old novels know that this gift also existed in ancient times.

The idea underlying the argument in this paragraph is that the institutions of a great society and their attendant rituals should be of such enduring rightness that no essential changes should be required for a hundred generations. I seem to have read something of the same tenor in eulogies of the British Constitution and in the speeches of certain Republican orators in the United States. The interesting thing is that Tzu Ssu's Amplifier—a Conservative, I think, and not Liberal or Labour—has laid it down that the administration of the true ruler must afford tangible evidence to the people as a whole that it is worthy of trust. Otherwise there is nothing that they can obey. This was the position which Rousseau held. It is one based on the simple logic of fact that what is white is white and what is black is black, and you cannot deceive the people. They know whether they are profiting or not from the institutions which affect them so intimately.

SECTION XVI. The Interaction of Politics and Natural Processes.

(c. 30.) Chung Ni handed on the (traditions of) Yao and Shun as if they had been his ancestors, and took Wen and Wu's laws as subjects of exposition. These conformed with the regularity of the stars above and fulfilled the laws of land and water below. They are to be compared with heaven and earth, for there is nothing which they do not hold and sustain, nothing which they do not cover and envelop. They are to be compared with the seasons in their interaction, with the light of the sun and the light of the moon giving place to each other. Thus all creatures were nourished alike with none injuring their fellows. All men pursued the Way alike with none contradicting it to another. By virtue of their lesser powers the streams flowed in their courses; and by virtue of their greater powers there were mighty transformations. This in them is that by which Heaven-and-Earth is supreme.

¶ It is not clear in the text whether the subject of this eulogy is Confucius or the sage-kings or their traditions and laws. The traditional interpretation has favoured Confucius, but I question whether in the third century B.C. the scholars were thinking of him in quite such an exalted fashion. Also the Amplifier has shown how it is *li*, the sacred institutions and their rituals, about which he is primarily concerned.

The word translated by 'laws' is not the ordinary one *fa*

which the Legalists used, but one which denotes the constitutory laws, the initial promulgations which Rousseau distinguished so clearly from ordinary laws.

The connection made between these laws and the processes of Nature may well have had a grossly superstitious side to them, and in other and later works the element of the miraculous is quite prominent. That is not apparent here; but rather a lofty kind of mysticism which believes that if man conforms his social institutions to the ways of Nature, he reaches the point where he can influence Nature. Thus, for example, Yü, the sage-king who saved men from devastating floods, is often represented as producing a marvellous harmony of interaction between Nature and man; but in the accounts of his labours there is no sign of the miraculous. He succeeded because he studied the lie of the land and the natural flow of water, and because he persisted with incredible patience.

SECTION XVII. In order to rule the Emperor must have Sage-like Qualities.

(c. 31.) It is only the man who is entirely sage-like in the Great Society who can be both brilliant in intellect and intuitively wise, and thus be adequate for being over all men: who can be magnanimous and tender-hearted, and thus be adequate for being king to all: who can be strong and determined, and thus be adequate for holding all in control: who can be outwardly composed and inwardly true, and thus be adequate for being revered: who can be cultured in mind and withdrawn into his studious thoughts, and thus be adequate for distinguishing between true and false. Like a fathomless deep spring, continually gushing forth and watering far and wide! Being all-embracing like heaven and deep as a spring from the abyss, when he appears, the people all revere him: when he speaks, they all trust him: when he acts, they all take delight in him. Thus it is that his fame spreads from end to end of the civilized world [lit. the Middle Kingdom] and even to the barbarian tribes. Wherever ships and carriages go, wherever the strength of man penetrates, wherever the canopy of heaven is overhead and the earth bears up the world, on whatever spot the sun and the moon shine and the frosts and dews fall, all who have blood and breath pay loving homage to him. And thus it may be said, he pairs with Heaven.

¶ The traditionalists are perhaps right in holding that the writer of these words had Confucius in the back of his mind. But it is surely doubtful whether he was thinking very closely of the Sage.

The First Emperor had his superstitious side and was surrounded by men, both office-seekers and magicians, who did their utmost to encourage him in that way. Tzu Ssu's Amplifier makes the counter-appeal as if he said to the Emperor, You are thinking that you *pei' T'ien* (pair with Heaven), but there is only one way by which a man can do that. In elaborating he shows his immense idealism. Yet, if we examine closely the combinations of qualities and their corresponding functions, a very clear strain of ethical common sense emerges. These are the functions and qualities which leadership entails. Plato in Athens found that he had to deal with this matter, and the result was his intensely idealistic picture of philosopher-kings. It is instructive that the Chinese thinker, faced with totalitarian conditions, envisaged the necessity for kindness and, as appeared in Section XV, for popular approval. The Greek thinkers, living in a democracy, envisaged an autocratic government.

SECTION XVIII. Tzu Ssu links Human Realness to the Spiritual Power of Heaven.

(c. 32.) It is only the man who is entirely real in his world of men who can make the warp and woof of the great fabric of civilized life, who can establish the great foundations of civilized society, and who can understand the nourishing processes of heaven and earth. Can there be any variableness in him? His human-heartedness how insistent! His depth how unfathomable! His super-humanness how overwhelming! Who is there who can comprehend this unless he possess acute intelligence and sage-like wisdom, unless he reach out to the spiritual power of Heaven!

¶ The Amplifier, as editor of Tzu Ssu's book, gives us here a passage which, as I have explained in Chapter IV of the Introduction, seems to be more like Tzu Ssu's writing than his own.

The passage fits on to the end of Section XI, making a good climax to it. It is difficult to believe that the passage is from the Amplifier. For one thing, there has already been in the previous section a very similar outburst over supreme personality. Why should there be a second? For another thing, the central idea of realness, which has vanished from the argument since Section XI, is suddenly reintroduced here.

Chu Hsi felt that this passage was the climax of the book. It certainly would be an effective one. The central idea is carried to the point where the supreme realness is seen to be beyond comprehension unless a man adds to his intelligence and knowledge an approach to that ultimate objective thing, the *te* (spiritual power) of Heaven. This fits with the first affirmation made about *ch'eng*, namely that reality is the characteristic of Heaven and coming-to-be-real the characteristic of man.

Since *te* so often has also the meaning of 'power of personality,' the reader with a Christian tradition may wonder whether *T'ien Te* here should not be rendered as 'Heaven's power of personality.' It would be interesting if it could be, but I doubt very much whether it can be. *T'ien*, as has already been said, appears in *The Mean-in-action* to be a Supreme Will ordering all things for man's good, expressing itself in high commissions to sage-like individuals, but there is no evidence that I know of beyond that outlined in the comment of Section IV for attaching personality in the Christian sense to the concept of Heaven. The impersonal 'spiritual power' is, in my judgment, more in harmony with *T'ien*.

SECTION XIX. The Amplifier reinforces Tzu Ssu's Argument.

(c. 33.) There is the expression in the *Book of Songs*: 'Over her embroidered robe she wears a simple cloak'; for she dislikes the display of the robe's elegance. Hence the Way of the true man is hidden from view yet daily more resplendent, whilst the untrue man takes the obvious path and daily goes more and more to ruin. The true man may seem tasteless, but people do not weary of him. He has simplicity along with great accomplishments, is thorough but all in accord with principle. He knows the nearness of the distant, that, indeed, the wind must come from somewhere, that the invisible must become visible. Such a man has the right to enter into spiritual power. As it is said in the *Book of Songs*: 'Without a word we seek the presence. During this time (of sacrifice) all quarrels are put aside.' Before the true monarch gives rewards for goodness, the people are already encouraged to be good. Before he punishes in his anger, they fear him in a way that no hatchets or battle-axes can make them fear. As it is said in the *Book of Songs*: 'Nothing is more resplendent than their spiritual power. The chieftains all pattern themselves on it.' Thus it is that the true monarch is true-hearted and reverent of spirit, and the world is at peace. As the saying is in the *Book of Songs*: 'I am moved by your spiritual power of understanding. You do not build your fame on empty show.' And the Master said: 'Of the means of transforming the people, the least is the bubble of fame.' And, again, in the *Book of Songs*: 'Spiritual power is weightless as a hair. Yet even a hair has a weight for comparison.' But 'the deeds of high Heaven are without sound and smell.' This is perfection.[1]

¶ The Amplifier's hand is again clearly at work. As in Section XII he reinforced the argument of Section XI with his own purpose in view, so here again he wants to make sure that Tzu Ssu's sublime conclusion shall be put into terms which will bring it home to the Emperor. It is significant, therefore, that whereas Section XVIII finishes with the spiritual power of Heaven without any reference in the section to governing, this section is entirely concerned with governing but finishes with Heaven and perfection. It is almost inevitable that when a redactor or amplifier inserts his own ideas alongside those of a great writer of an earlier age, the discovery of this fraud, as it may seem, should create a prejudice in our minds against the presumptuous fellow. In this case of *The Mean-in-action*, such a prejudice should be sharply disciplined. In the first place, amplifying was the common practice of that time, and, in spite

---

[1] There is a Taoistic touch to this end which, in my judgment, suggests a later origin for the passage than Tzu Ssu's age. Han Confucianist writings often show this, and Hsun Ch'ing's book (third century B.C., *med.*) shows Taoist influence very clearly. Cp. also *Record of Rites* (*Sacred Books of the East*, vol. xxviii, p. 279).

of the awful confusions it has created for the historians of classical Chinese thought, we have in the last resort to be thankful that there were men who dared enough to keep the earlier works in circulation. In the second place, this Amplifier of Tzu Ssu was a man of noble convictions, and, I would urge, extraordinary courage. For here I must state my final conclusion from a historical point of view. It is, as I have suggested in more than one comment, that this Confucianist of the First Emperor's time made this combination of Tzu Ssu's ideas and his own with the direct intention of presenting it to that grim Führer-like person, the First Emperor. He hoped to convert him from his mechanized notions of society and inhuman treatment of men.

If this interpretation should prove trustworthy, then we have to face the fact that the Emperor was not converted by this appeal or by any of the others which we have reason to believe were made by the Confucianists of that time. Further, it is stated in the *Record of History* by Ssu-ma Tan and Ssu-ma Ch'ien (c. 100 B.C.) that four hundred and sixty Ju (scholars) were buried alive for showing disapproval of the Emperor's actions. On the basis of this information, it would be likely that our friend, Tzu Ssu's Amplifier, paid the penalty of his courage with his life. If that happened, it was, in a sense, a bad day for him when he read and accepted those words of Tzu Ssu's: 'There are five things which concern everybody in the Great Society, as also do the three means by which these five things are accomplished . . . knowledge, human-heartedness, and fortitude.' But it was a good day for the Chinese people, and may be for the world. Knowledge of noble principles, even when coupled with faith in Heaven or in the Providence of God, does not of itself produce the victory of the good in this world as it is. Neither does knowledge plus human-heartedness faithfully embodied in common action. But a case may be made out for the belief that if fortitude be added, the combination of the three is irresistible. Such a belief entails belief in Tzu Ssu's proposition that there is an absolute called Heaven and a relative counterpart to it in man, a quality of coming-to-be-realness which exists effectively in some men, not in others. The belief also entails a faith that the men who have this realness are not obliterated when they die. Their power of personality continues to exist in the society which they served among the men with whom they were and are in real relation. The Great Society, civilization in the true sense, cannot exist unless this be so.

'THE GREAT LEARNING'

The text used is the same one which I have used for the translation of *The Mean-in-action*, namely the *Sung Pen Shih San Ching* as found in Juan Yüan's famous edition at the beginning of the nineteenth century: cp. his *Chu Shu Fu Chiao K'an Chi*. There is ground for regarding this text as the most reliable version we have of *The Great Learning* as it reached the Sung scholars.

I have come to the conclusion that there was no need for such elaborate changes as Ch'eng Yi-ch'uan and Chu Hsi made in the earlier part of this version. I venture to urge that their minds were sharpened to a more analytical edge than the mind of the author: that their powers of literary criticism were too refined. Where they thought there was expounding of illustrious *te*, of renovating the people, etc., the author was merely pursuing the tenor of one great, simple thought that the flowering of personality is the root of all good, and that this flowering involves extending knowledge, knowledge of man in all his ethical significance, to the furthest extent possible. In avowing this position I confess to 'the Learned' that I am under the influence of the Intuitionist school. That is so to a certain extent. It seems to me in its more sober moods to have thought good, scholarly common sense. On the other hand, Chu Hsi was, of course, quite right in transposing the section 'On Making Purposes Genuine' to where he did. Once that is done, however, surely the text should remain unchanged except for one addition, namely, the four words, *so wei chih pen*. I submit that these words got omitted by the copyists after they had written *tzu wei chih pen*. These added words are the introductory phrase which begins the first section of explanation after the statement of the theme. That statement ends with: 'This is to be described as knowing the root,' and the new section starts with: 'As for what is described as knowing the root.' In this way the whole series of quotations down to the one from Confucius about being an arbitrator is to be taken as one section which conforms to the literary pattern of the book. That pattern is each section begins with a '*So wei . . .*' and, with the exception of two, ends with '*Tzu wei. . . .*'

It was while I was reading Mao Ch'i-ling's *Ta Hsueh Wen Cheng* that this solution of the problem came to me, so that I owe the idea, at any rate in part, to him. That I should then have fallen into the same sin as the Ch'eng-Chu philosophers, and that he would have regarded my interference with the sacred text as outrageous presumption, does not affect the fact. My translation, therefore, is along the lines of this solution and embodies the four words, *so wei chih pen*. In order to help the student-reader I have put Chu Hsi's chapter and paragraph numbers in parentheses. These correspond to the divisions in Legge's translation in his *Chinese Classics*, vol. i, Clarendon Press, 1893.

SECTION I. A General Statement of the Theme of the Book.

(*The original part by Confucius*)

The Way of learning to be great consists in shining with the illustrious power of moral personality, in making a new people, in abiding in the highest goodness. To know one's abiding place leads to fixity of purpose, fixity of purpose to calmness of mind, calmness of mind to serenity of life, serenity of life to careful consideration of means, careful consideration of means to the achievement of the end.

¶ The reader has become familiar in *The Mean-in-action* with the careful building up of chains of inferences. He will find in this book, as for example here, the same attention to logic. The recurrence of these chains plus other features in the style point to the work having been written with a special purpose in view to its being learnt off by heart (cp. Introduction, Chapter IV), as, indeed, many millions of schoolboys did learn it from the thirteenth to the twentieth century.

Things have their roots and branches, human affairs their endings as well as beginnings. So to know what comes first and what comes afterwards leads one near to the Way. The men of old who wished to shine with the illustrious power of personality throughout the Great Society, first had to govern their own states efficiently. Wishing to do this, they first had to make an ordered harmony in their own families. Wishing to do this, they first had to cultivate their individual selves (*hsiu shen*). Wishing to do this, they first had to put their minds right. Wishing to do this, they first had to make their purposes genuine. Wishing to do this, they first had to extend their knowledge to the utmost. Such extension of knowledge consists in appreciating the nature of things. For with the appreciation of the nature of things knowledge reaches its height. With the completion of knowledge purposes become genuine. With purposes genuine the mind becomes right.

With the mind right the individual self comes into flower (*shen hsiu*). With the self in flower the family becomes an ordered harmony. With the families ordered harmonies the State is efficiently governed. With States efficiently governed the Great Society is at peace.

¶ The setting forth of the eight steps from illustrious *te* to the appreciation of things, first from the historical angle as verified facts and then starting from the other end as general propositions, is of very great interest. The author obviously is set on making his argument doubly clear and impressive.

'What comes first and what comes afterwards': this may well mean what we mean by the moralistic phrase (putting first things first); but I am inclined to think that 'what are causes and what effects' is the more likely meaning.

Ko wu (appreciation of the nature of things), the phrase over which there has been more bitter and prolonged controversy than any other in the history of Chinese scholarship. Legge's 'the investigation of things' follows Chu Hsi's interpretation, but 'investigation' conveys an idea of scientific examination which is, I suggest, alien to the mind of the author. Therefore I substitute 'appreciation,' a term native to the field of aesthetics and conveying the idea of instructive responsiveness to the significance of the said 'things.' These 'things' I take to be the *shih* (matters)—as the *K'ung Yin-ta* of the T'ang era called them—which are set forth in Section II below. Nevertheless, in a general loose sense, not in Chu Hsi's precise one (cp. Introduction, Chapter II), the author may surely be regarded as wanting to convey the necessity there is for understanding the nature of things.

Hsiu shen (cp. *Mean-in-action, passim*): the sublime, if dangerous imperative of the Confucianist ethic. In later phases of Confucianist thought the phrase came to have strongly disciplinary significance. I doubt whether it had this in the early days of its use. The form of the character, is, I suggest, illuminating: *yu* 'that by which,' 'process by which,' plus *shan* 'the plumage of a bird full-grown.' The English metaphor is in relation to flowers, not birds, hence my translation.

Thus from the Son of Heaven down to the common people there is unity in this; that for everybody the bringing of the individual self to flower is to be taken as the root.

(Since that is so), for the root to be out of order and the branches to be in order is an impossibility. For a man to despise what he should respect and then be respected for having what he despises, is contrary to human experience. This is to be described as knowing the root.

¶ In the comments I shall largely refrain from making cross-references to *The Mean-in-action*. That there was a fundamental unity of purpose and belief between that book and this one will become abundantly clear. Thus, the emphasis the author here lays on the fact that the successful conduct of the life of the community depends on the individual, is precisely the emphasis which Tzu Ssu laid. Both men were profoundly concerned with the flowering of the individual, whether he be 'the rich man in his castle or the poor man at his gate.' It is for this reason, as much as any, that a western reader may find a Chinese classic giving food for thought at the present time.

SECTION II. On Knowing the Root.
(c. 3, par. 4.) As for what is described as knowing the root,[1] this means the height of knowledge. For in the *Book of Songs* are the words:

> See there, the Ch'i river with its winding course,
> Its bamboos all lush and green!
> Even so our accomplished prince!
> The bone is carved and the ivory polished;
> The jade is cut and granite ground smooth.
> So he, like the music of strings yet with a martial air,
> Stern yet debonair.
> So accomplished a prince,
> Ever to be held in memory.

That 'carving and polishing' means learning. That 'cutting and grinding' means the cultivation of the self. 'Like the music of strings,' so he trembles within himself. 'Stern yet debonair,' so he is the very pattern of majesty. 'Ever to be held in memory,' so abounding power of personality and the height of goodness are what the common people can never forget. As the *Book of Songs* has it: 'How

---

[1] I propose the addition to the text of this introductory phrase. The previous paragraph having ended with 'This is to be described as knowing the root (*tzu wei chih pen*),' it would be easy for a copyist to omit *so wei chih pen*.

the kings of old are borne in mind.' The true man deems
worthy those whom they deemed worthy: the common
people take pleasure in the pleasures and gain profit from
the profits which they made. Thus it is that although he
is gone from the world he is not forgotten.

¶ I think we must visualize the situation described in Chapter
IV of the Introduction, a tutor preparing lessons for his pupils,
a group of young lordlings, amongst whom were one or more
marked out as likely to succeed to the headship of the State.
The teaching method is good. This tutor picks certain passages
from the *Book of Songs*, the *Book of Documents*, legendary history,
etc., and his pupils are set to learn them. Presumably their
teacher enlarged on the meaning of each passage, and the heroic
qualities of the man described.

As an illustration of the way in which a Great Tradition is built
up by the enrichment of language, the four words *ch'ieh ts'o, tso
mo* (carving and polishing, cutting and grinding) became stock
expressions for that shaping and refinement of character which
comes, or rather should come, from a liberal education, and the
disciplinary experiences of life in the family and society. The
user of the expression, in whatever age, had the ethical in mind:
but the ethical was enriched by association with the aesthetic.

In *The Mean-in-action* (Section V) it was the descendants of
the man of outstanding personality who preserved his memory.
Here it is the people generally. The point is the same, of
course: the continuous existence of the spiritual power of the
man who 'is gone from the world.'

(c. 1.) In the *K'ang Kao* it is said: 'He has the gifts of
illustrious power of personality. In the *T'ai Chia* it is
said: 'He guards this illustrious charge from Heaven.'
In the *Ti Tien* it is said: 'He has the gifts for shedding lustre
on his outstanding power of personality.' These three are
cases of the self giving lustre.

¶ 'Illustrious,' 'shedding lustre,' this is the connecting thought
here: compare the opening sentence of the book. It is very
possible that the author included the idea of bright intelligence
in his use of *ming* here. He did not approve of the high-
brows of his day, but he had a great respect for true intelligence,

and he is here teaching his pupils the basic things an intelligent man must know.

(c. 2.) On King T'ang's bath-tub there was an inscription: 'If on one day there may be a renovation, then every day there may be, indeed, daily there must be.' So in the *K'ang Kao* it is said: 'Making a new people' and in the *Book of Songs* is the saying: 'The fief which Chou held was an ancient one, but the charge from Heaven was new.' The true man, therefore, in everything uses his supreme endeavours.

¶ T'ang, the sage-king, founder of the previous regime to the Chou, was often spoken of as 'the Successful T'ang.' He is described in the *Book of Documents* as the man who always rose before daylight and meditated as he watched for the dawn. The *T'ai Chia* quoted above describes how his chief minister, according to one legend originally his cook, saved his young successor from evil courses.

It is impossible to overestimate the influence which the idea of a new charge from Heaven has had on the Chinese people. The latest instance of this was in the first decade of this century when it was coupled by the reformers with the other idea alongside of it in this passage: 'making a new people.' This was the watchword of Dr. Sun Yat Sen and his party when the Republic was founded in 1912. It is to be heard to-day in West China, where men spur themselves to the task of 'Reconstruction during Resistance.'

(c. 3, par. 1.) In the *Book of Songs* it is said: 'The royal demesne of a thousand *li* is where the people are really at rest.' In the *Book of Songs* it is said: '*Ming-mang* goes the oriole's song, as it rests on a corner of a mound'; and the Master said: 'As to resting, the bird knows where it can rest—is it right for a man to be less than a bird?'

¶ The 'at rest' and 'resting,' as the 'abiding' in the next quotation and the 'abiding' at the beginning of Section I, are all the same Chinese word *chih*. Purists in language and thought have a right to criticize a language which is prone to this kind of word play. But it has its value. Confucius's gentle sarcasm—

or perhaps it is a severe one—contrasts with Mo Ti's bludgeoning description of the 'gentlemen' of the world as tigers and wolves.

(c. 3, par. 2.) In the *Book of Songs* it is said:

> Hail to King Wen
> And the glorious homage he paid to abiding!
> As a monarch he abode in human-heartedness,
> As a minister he abode in reverence,
> As a son he abode in filial piety,
> As a father he abode in kindness,
> With his fellow countrymen he abode in good faith.

(c. 4.) The Master said: 'As an arbitrator in men's quarrels I am no better than other men. Inevitably so! If only there could be no cases for arbitration.' Then inhuman men would be barred from acting out their (inhuman) contentions, and people's private-mindedness would be greatly checked.

(c. 5.) All this means knowing the root.

¶ Confucius's point would appear to be that under certain conditions, for example in the heat of litigation, abiding in goodness is to all intents and purposes impossible. The dice are too heavily loaded in favour of men who will go to any lengths. That being so, even the best of arbitrators cannot achieve any real success. The only remedy, therefore, is moral education of such a kind that people will not quarrel in this bitter way.

Section III. On Making Purposes Genuine.

(c. 6.) What is described as 'making one's purposes genuine' is as follows. Beware of self-deception. It is to be compared to hating a bad smell and loving a lovely sight; this is what is called self-fulfilment. Thus it is that the true man is sure to be on guard when he is alone. The man who is not true in his privacy, has the habit of setting no limit to the badness of his actions. Then when he comes into the presence of a true man he is abashed. He conceals his bad qualities and displays his good. But he gains nothing by doing so, for (under these conditions) a man sees himself as if he saw his own liver and reins. This means that what is really within will take on form without. That is why the true man is sure to be on guard when he is alone. As Master Tseng said: 'How awe-inspiring must be what many eyes gaze at and many hands point to!' 'As riches adorn a house, so moral power adorns a man. The mind is enlarged, the limbs are at ease. This is why a true man is sure to make his purposes genuine.

¶ The Chinese character translated by 'genuine' is *cheng*, the same character which was used by Tzu Ssu when he wanted to denote reality and realness.

I confess I find the sentiments quoted from Master Tseng, presumably the great filial-pietist, a little prosy. But the beginning of the section is stimulating. To begin with, there is no reference to God's laws or what is enjoined in some sacred book, in short, no appeal to authority of any kind except the interim authority of a man's instinctive dislike of a bad smell and love of a lovely sight. To this is added later the uncontrollable reaction the untrue man has when he meets a true man. He makes a hasty appearance of goodness, but all to no purpose, for the very pretence reveals to him his own hidden self. This is a very discerning piece of introspection, in spite of certain criticisms which may be made. Thus, for example, a man cannot see his own inside. True! But if he did see it, he could not begin to pretend that it was other than what it is. Not with his own inside, surely! It is on this level that the author thought, and so became convinced that when a man makes up his mind to pursue any purpose, he can, if he wishes, always tell whether it is genuine or not. If he does deceive himself, he will in time run up against a true man who will undeceive him. That being the position taken up, it is interesting that our good teacher does not sum up with what seems to be the obvious moralistic conclusion, namely, that there is no excuse for purposes not being genuine.

SECTION IV. On the Relation of the Rectification of the Mind to Cultivation of the Self.

(c. 7.) As for the meaning of 'the cultivation of the self consists in the rectification of the mind,' if the self is angry about anything, or frightened, or delighted over anything, or unhappily perturbed about anything, in each case it follows that it cannot get itself right. When the mind is away, we gaze at things and do not see them, sounds come to our ears and we do not hear them, we eat and do not discern the flavours. This is what is meant by 'the cultivation of the self consists in the rectification of the mind.'

¶ The author dealt in the last section with purposes without relating them to the consequence he had laid down, namely, the rectification of the mind. From here on he deals with each step, in this case the cultivation or flowering of the self depending on a man's obtaining a right mind. About this 'self,' we had it in *The Mean-in-action* and here it is in *The Great Learning*. *Shen* in some contexts in classical Chinese unmistakably means 'the body,' the trunk as distinct from the limbs. But in other contexts it equally unmistakably means the self. Perhaps the image of the trunk gave rise to the metaphorical usage, people thinking of the main part of their selves as *shen* in distinction from outlying less representative parts of themselves. The reader may well ask what the author meant by the 'mind.' To such a question I cannot give a satisfactory answer. I can only say that generally speaking at that time they spoke of the *hsin*, the character the early form of which shows that it was a picture-graph of the heart, as the thing with which men thought. Also there are passages which say that the *hsin*, not the passions, should be in control of a man. The passions or emotions were not associated with the heart in the way that western popular pyschology has associated them. The Taoists became convinced that the right aim for a man was to reduce the passions either to a bare minimum or to non-existence. The Confucianists were less radical in their thought on the matter; but they none the less held, as our author does here, that to be under the influence of the passions meant that the mind was not in control. On the other hand, to draw the conclusion that the mind and its thoughts were identified with reason is, in my judgment, not warranted, unless an extremely wide meaning is given to the concept of reason. Cp. the next section. May we not say that the teacher wanted his pupils to realize that this business of rectifying the mind is not such a simple business as they might think, and that at the same time it is a *sine que non* in the cultivation of the self? With this good approach which he makes to the problem of the relation between knowledge and morality, it is disappointing that he does not go any further. For closer thinking on that relation we have to go to Hsun Ch'ing of the third century B.C.

SECTION V. On the Relation of the Cultivation of the Self to the Bringing of an Ordered Harmony in the Family.

(c. 8.) As for the meaning of 'the bringing of the members of the family into an ordered harmony consists in cultivating the self,' men are prejudiced about those whom they love, prejudiced about those whom they hate, prejudiced about those whom they revere, prejudiced about those whom they pity, prejudiced about those whom they despise. There are very few people in the world who are awake to the evil in the object of their liking and awake to the attractiveness in the object of their dislike. Hence, as the proverb puts it: 'Men are not aware of the evil of their sons or of the fertility of their field.' This means that there can be no bringing of the members of the family into an ordered harmony unless there is cultivation of the self.

¶ The treatment here, as in Section IV, is surprisingly scrappy, considering that the subject, the flowering of the self and the family, is one about which a Confucianist might be expected to have a good deal to say. As a matter of fact, the author is more expansive on the family in the next section. Here we must perhaps remember that if the author was teaching young lordlings, he could not expect them to have much interest in refinements about the cultivation of the self. The one point he does make is the extremely practical one with which his pupils would b eonly too familiar. To judge from the *Tso Chuan*, domestic peace in the various courts was constantly being shattered by the lengths to which personal preferences and personal animosities were carried.

SECTION VI. On the Relation between Bringing the Family into an Ordered Harmony and the Efficient Ruling of the State.

(c. 9.) As for the meaning of 'the efficient ruling of a

State of necessity consists in bringing its families into an ordered harmony,' it is not the case that a man can fail in instilling good principles into his own family and, at the same time, succeed in instilling those principles into men outside it. Thus it is that a true man without going outside his family brings good principles into being throughout the country. Filial piety is the means by which the prince is served. Deference to an elder brother is the means by which the elder generation is served. The exercise of parental kindness is the means by which a whole population is influenced. In the *K'ang Kao* it is said: 'Act as if you were watching over an infant.' If your mind is truly set on your action, although you may miss your mark, you will not go far astray. A young woman has never had to learn to suckle an infant before she gets married.

¶ This passage illustrates a tendency in thinkers of the classical era to find in Nature's instincts a sure guide to man in his quest for true happiness. It was assumed by Confucianists—though not by Taoists—that that happiness could only come in community of living. Hence those instincts which led to the building up of a family life were felt to be fundamentally significant. That they were not in themselves a sufficient guide is part of the theme of *The Great Learning*. Community in living depends on the cultivated moral self, the individual in flower. Once that flowering is achieved man is on the way to happiness. But his happiness cannot exist apart from the family. Indeed, it cannot come in the larger society of the country unless it first comes in the family. So the Great Tradition of the Chinese people would have us believe.

If one family be human-hearted, human-heartedness will grow in the whole country. If the members of one family give way to each other, the spirit of giving way will grow in the whole country. If one man[1] be incontinently

---

[1] It is possible, though I think very doubtful, that his 'one man' may refer to the king. There came a time when kings officially referred to themselves as 'I, the one man' (cp. *Record of Rites, Yü Ts'ao, ad fin.*), but I am not persuaded that this was before the time of Shih Huang Ti.

wicked, he will cause anarchy in the whole country. The mechanism of the situation is like that. This means that one remark may throw public business into disorder, or one man may consolidate a country.

It was through being human-hearted that Yao and Shun were the leaders in the Great Society. The people followed (*ts'ung*) their example. It was through being oppressors that Chieh and Chow were the leaders in the Great Society: the people obeyed (*ts'ung*) them. But since the actions they commanded were contrary to what they liked to do themselves, there was no (real) obedience. Thus it is that what the true man has in himself, that he can require from others: what he has not in himself, that he cannot require from others: there never has been a man who had no store of reciprocity in himself and yet was able to communicate it to other men. Hence the ruling of a state consists in ordered harmony in the family.

¶ According to the *Analects* (XV, 23) a disciple asked Confucius if there was one word which might serve as a practical rule for life, and Confucius replied: 'Will reciprocity do? What you do not want done to yourself, do not hand out to others.'

Again the impression is received of a man thinking in profoundly realistic fashion, though I suppose that it is arguable that only an ethical idealist would commit himself to the general statement: 'There never has been a man . . .' Obviously, nobody is in a position to make such a statement on the basis of verified fact, and our author might have been better advised to say that it is self-evident. That is pretty much what he means, and on the face of it his statement would appear to be incontestable. Further, when the philosophical reader was perusing the section on reality in substance or in relation in Chapter II of the Introduction, he may have had serious qualms as to whether the classical Chinese mind had sufficient understanding of the logician's Law of Identity. In the face of the statement here any such qualms may perhaps be allayed. Our author seems quite clear, at any rate, in the field of moral pyschology, that a man cannot give to another what he does not possess himself. That is, the A kind of man cannot at one and the same time be the B kind, nor the B kind of man the A kind.

In the *Book of Songs* is the saying:

> How charming the peach-tree
> Its leaves thickly massed!
> The bride is coming to her home:
> The bride will rightly order her household.[1]

True! Order your household and then you can teach good principles to influence the nation. In the *Book of Songs* is the saying: 'With elder brother's duty done, with younger brother's duty done.' True. Fulfil your duties as elder and younger brother, and then you can teach good principles to the nation. In the *Book of Songs* is the saying: 'His ways are faultless. He puts the four fiefs to rights.' True! The ruler as a father, as a son, as a younger brother, as an elder brother, first rises to the level of being a model, then the people come to be modelled on him. This is the meaning of 'the ruling of a state consists in ordered harmony in the family.'

¶ The last two quotations are from court eulogies, so that the author may be assumed, without his explicitly saying so, to have rulers and their families in mind. The first quotation, from an ode of welcome to a bride, only probably has an aristocratic source. Its simplicity makes one wonder whether it does not represent the popular feeling about a bride. The *Book of Songs* is full of romance in the modern western newspaper sense (cp. Mr. Waley's *The Book of Songs*), and the comparison here of the bride with peach blossom needs no explanation to the reader. But the picture is also of a robust young woman, well trained in housewifely duties and able to manage the serving-men and maids in the house. The picture of a downtrodden daughter-in-law, which some western residents in China have popularized, is not by any means the only side to the life of young married women. It is well to remember that the bride had her status in the family, as is clear from this poem which has survived for 2,500 years, and she could in time achieve a quite matriarchal position also. It is part of the Chinese Great Tradition to recognize not only an ethical importance in family life, but also a great aesthetic charm. The family stirs their sense of poetry.

[1] Cp. Appendix on Rousseau and Nature in Family Relations.

SECTION VII. On the Relation between the Government of States and Universal Peace.

The argument in this section is an extensive one and is divisible into five subsections.

(1) The Way of the Measuring Square.

(pars. 1, 2.) As to the meaning of 'the attainment of peace in the Great Society consists in the efficient government of the States,' if those in high places treat old age as old age should be treated, the people develop the filial spirit. If those in high places treat their seniors as seniors should be treated, the people develop the younger-brotherly spirit. If they have pity on orphans, the people will not go counter to them. Thus there is for the true man the Way of the Measuring Square.[1] What a man dislikes in those above him, he must not bring to bear on those beneath him. What he dislikes in those beneath him, he must not bring to the service of those above him. What he dislikes in his forbears, he must not do in advance for his descendants. What he would dislike in his descendants, he must not do as following his forbears. The treatment which he dislikes from (his neighbours on) the right, he must not give to (those on) the left. The treatment which he dislikes from (his neighbours on) the left, he must not give to (those on) the right. This is what is meant by the Way of the Measuring Square.

¶ Confucius, as we have seen above, is on record as having given *shu* (reciprocity) as a principle which should be practised throughout life. The connection of *shu* with lifelong observance presumably refers to the changing conditions into which a man comes: in his youth a son and under the authority of the state officials, later in life a father and possibly an official, or even exercising the supreme authority of a ruling monarch. In every case the treatment which a man does not like for himself, he is not to hand out to other people. Beyond this point there is no indication that Confucius felt called to define the scope of *shu*. In this he belonged to the company of the great

[1] The measuring square was a carpenter's tool. This metaphor for the principle of reciprocity is not found in the *Analects*. Our author may be the man who coined the expression.

religious leaders and ethical reformers, the men who discovered great liberating principles and, being liberated themselves, were not tempted to turn those principles into enslaving sets of rules. The disciple's mind is only too often not a liberated mind, particularly when his position is that of a pedagogue. In the passage before us we can see the temptation at work to elaborate and to mechanize. The fate of this principle has been a very different one from the principle, for example, of filial piety which, in course of time, became as much a soul-destroying as a life-giving influence. The worst that can be said of *shu* in the history of Chinese society is that it made good men too cautious about offending others; the best, that the Chinese people generally have been the world's best exponents of the Greek ethical concept of sweet reasonableness.

(2) What being Father and Mother to the People entails. (pars. 3–6). In the *Book of Songs* is the saying: 'Blessings on our true man, father and mother to his people.' To like what the people like and to hate what the people hate, this is the meaning of being father and mother. As in the *Book of Songs*:

> That South Mountain with its beetling crags!
> The height of it before our eyes!
> So the Grand Master
> In his overwhelming might!
> Not one can take his eyes from him.

True! The man with a country in his charge cannot afford not to be cautious. If he leaves that true path, he becomes the world's criminal. Again, as the *Book of Songs* says:

> Before they lost their people's (hearts)
> The Yin kings stood at God's right hand,
> The Yin kings stand before our eyes (as proof):
> God's high commission is hard to keep.

It is that: win the people, and the country is won: lose the people, and the country is lost. This is why the true man is first concerned with the power of moral personality. Possessing the power in himself, he possesses men. Possessing men, he possesses the soil. Possessing the soil, he possesses wealth. Possessing wealth, he possesses the means of governing.

¶ That a king is the observed of all and therefore bound to be doubly cautious must have been the commonplace of most royal tutors in Europe, but one may doubt whether a royal pupil in the West has ever been taught that it was his business to love what the people loved and hate what they hated. There is a good deal else to be taken into account alongside of this statement, e.g. that the Chou society was essentially an aristocratic, not a democratic, one. But these political facts only throw up this statement into sharper relief. Behind it lies the belief in the significance of natural instincts. This, however, is not enough to account for it. There must also be something approaching the conviction which Mencius was the first to have, namely, that man has a natural aptitude for goodness. There is no trace of this belief in *The Great Learning*, although, as was said of Confucius in Chapter III of the Introduction, the tendency of thought was in the direction of Mencius's theory. In the *Book of Documents*, the authentic parts of which must be assumed to be the work of the Chou royal historiographers, this sentiment about the people's loving and hating is also to be found. There is also the following: 'Heaven sees as the people see, Heaven hears as the people hear.' This is the Chinese version of *Vox populi, vox Dei*.

(3) Power of Personality is the Root, Wealth is the Branch.

(pars. 7-11.) This moral power is the root: wealth is but a branch. If the root be discounted and the branch be prized, there will be quarrelling, and the people will be incited to steal. This is why the people will disperse if the wealth be amassed in the ruler's hands, and why the people will mass round the ruler if the wealth be dispersed among them. And if the ruler's words go forth in injustice it is the reason why injustice will come home to roost. If injustice enters (the palace) with the produce of the country, injustice will take that produce away. It is said in the *K'ang Kao*: 'The charge from Heaven itself is not unchangeable.' This means that goodness brings it to a man, and evil takes it away from him.

¶ As far as I know, the theory which I have advocated (*vide* Introduction, Chapter IV) as to the date of *The Great Learning* has not been advocated before. A substantial part of the proof of this theory is the evidence I find in these three subsections. *The Great Learning* gives me the impression from the beginning of having been written by a man conscious that the principles in which he believed were being attacked. There is a clarity and pungency about his affirmations, a marking of contrasted behaviours, which could hardly have been attained by a pious idealistic scholar just meditating on the good life for man. This feature does not necessarily point to the book being written in Shang Yang's age, but when we come to these last paragraphs the situation is different. There is, for one thing, the vastly disproportionate length of the sections, a feature not wholly to be accounted for by the theory that the book was a series of lessons for young sprigs of nobility being prepared for high office in the State. For another thing, there are statements in these last paragraphs which may naturally be interpreted as rejoinders to the reported deeds and sayings of Shang Yang. Thus according to the *Shang Tzu Book*, it was the business of the Government to make the people do what they hated, namely, to work. Again, the end of government was wealth and power at the headquarters of the State. Shang Yang scoffed at the very idea of moral power. And again, there is the curious reference by our author to the ruler's words going forth in injustice (*p'e*). Shang Yang scoffed at the Confucianists' passion for 'talking.' He maintained that it did not matter what rulers said. What they did counted. So long as the law was clear and was rigorously enforced any injustice in it did not matter.

(4) Human-heartedness Essential.

(pars. 12–23.) It is said in the *Book of Ch'u*: 'The State of Ch'u has nothing it considers precious except its good men. Them it holds precious.' Uncle Fan said: 'As exiles there is nothing we count precious, only to be human-hearted to our kin.' In the *Ch'in Shih* it is said: 'If I have but one minister, a man with no guile in him, having no special skill, but open-hearted and showing this in his demeanour, welcoming another man's skill as if it were his own, in his heart no less than in his speech hailing genius in other men, and thus able to make way for them so that they can protect my descendants and my people—if I have this, how great is the gain. If, however, my minister be jealous of another's skill and go on to hate him: if he thwart the man of genius and block his way to advancement so that he is unable to guard my descendants and my people, how great is the peril.' The human-hearted man, he alone can send such a man packing, driving him out among the barbarian tribes, refusing to have him living alongside in the Middle Kingdom. This is the meaning of 'only the human-hearted man can love men, only he can hate men.' You may discover a man of worth and be unable to employ him, that is fate. But to discover a bad man (to be in office) and be unable to remove and banish him; that is your own fault. For to love what men hate and to hate what men love, this is an outrage on human nature, and disaster inevitably falls on such an individual. Thus it is that the true man has a supremely right Way. With devotion and good faith he is sure to succeed in it. With arrogance and dissipation, he is sure to fail.

¶ From 384 B.C. on, Ch'u State grew in military power and prestige among the other states. It is possible that *The Great Learning* was written shortly after 384 B.C. For in that year Ch'u attacked and destroyed the powerful State of Yueh; and it would be like our teacher-author to draw his pupil's attention to a very different expression of the Ch'u political mind from that shown in the discreditable and unfortunately successful operations against Yueh. The *Ch'u Ssu* is one of the books in the *Kuo Yü*, a work probably composed in the third century B.C. and consisting of passages from the annals of the various states.

This Fan was uncle to a duke of Tsin. He was exiled by his father wrongfully. It is perhaps significant that a duke of Ch'in—Shang Yang was Prime Minister in Ch'in—offered to help Fan and his friends to get back by force to Tsin.

The *Ch'in Shih* (Oath of Ch'in) is the final book in the *Book of Documents*. Taking each of the sentiments expressed in this paragraph, we find that the bad qualities fit very closely with what we know of Shang Yang's career. The whole quotation is extraordinarily pointed, and whether *The Great Learning* was written before or after Shang Yang's death (?338 B.C.), there is a gruesome aptness in the final prophecy of calamity. He died fighting, pursued by his enemies to his last lair. Nothing would satisfy them but to tear his body to pieces and to exterminate his whole family. So Ssu-ma Ch'ien's biography of him has put on record. He was an exact illustration of what happens to a man who loves what the people hate and hates what the people love.

(5) On the National Scale Justice is Gain.[1]

For the creation of wealth there is a supremely right Way. If those who create the wealth be many, those who consume it few, and if the accumulating departments be zealous, the spending departments economical, then there will be a permanent sufficiency of wealth.

For the human-hearted man wealth is the means by which the individual self is expanded. For the non-human-hearted man the individual is a tool for the expansion of wealth. There never has been a case in which those in high places were devoted to human-heartedness and those beneath them were not devoted to justice. There never has been a case in which there was devotion to justice and State affairs failed of completion. There never has been a case in which (in these circumstances) there was opposition to the wealth being in the Government's storehouses.

Meng Hsien Tzu said: 'If you have the status of keeping a horse and carriage, you do not keep a check on fowls and pigs. The great family with its stores of ice does not tend sheep and cattle.' So also the great house of a hundred chariots does not keep a special officer for collecting taxes. With such an officer, in what way is it better than employing a robbing expert? This means that on the national scale it is not gain that is (real) gain, but justice. The man at the head of a country's administration who is only concerned with wealth and expenditure is himself a base fellow. He may think he is doing good, but his ways of getting things done are those of a base fellow. Calamity from Heaven and injury from men both ensue, and although there may be good men in the country, they can do nothing to stop this. This means that on the national scale gain is not (real) gain: justice is gain.

[1] I use 'justice' for *yi*, justice in the wide Platonic sense with its implication that righteousness has at its centre the idea of equity and fair dealing.

¶ Meng Hsien Tzu was a minister of Lu State in the generation before Confucius. There were suggestions about even in his day that feudal administration should be tightened up and taxation systematized. He was opposed to this on good old-fashioned grounds, and maintained that a gentleman did not concern himself with these huckstering methods of making his fief pay. He had the same semi-benevolent, semi-paternal attitude towards the lower classes as was shown by certain county ladies in England early in the twentieth century who regarded Lloyd George's scheme of state insurance for servants as an outrage on their social honour. The social grades depicted in this quotation are obvious, but the reference to ice perhaps needs explanation. Only a really wealthy family would have sufficient labour at its command to enable it to have an ice-house excavated in which winter ice could be stored for summer use. In the serf's calendar of work in the *Book of Songs* there is a description of the serfs opening up the ice-house when the time came. The number of war chariots a feudatory could produce determined his position in the feudal scale.

Shang Yang made wealth and a war machine the root, whilst his Confucianist opponent made them the branches of national life. In those days the State with a large number of war chariots was a first-class power, the State with a less number a second-class power. Whether war chariots or ships, the facts are the same. Britain can face a continent marshalled against her because she has money in England and dispersed all about the world (cp. Subsection 3): above all, because she has a great Navy and Merchant Service.

Going back two centuries to the time when Britain's naval power first made phenomenal advances, we find an England which was largely like that with which Meng Hsien Tzu was familiar, a semi-feudal society with its aristocracy and its merchants and farmers and labourers. The great families began to invest their money in industrial enterprises, not only at home but also in the seafaring enterprises which characterized the eighteenth century. In other words, the feudal mind which Meng Hsien Tzu's words exemplify changed to the modern mind. The gentleman did concern himself with 'fowls and pigs . . . sheep and cattle' (or the modern dividend-producing equivalents). So also in Japan of the mid-nineteenth century: the Samurai discarded their feudal privileges and were made the military guardians of the nation's honour with the unwritten law that they should not embroil themselves in trade. To-day, the worst of the racketeers in Manchuria and North China, and in the Yangtse valley, are the descendants of these same Samurai, the men engaged in military service.

It would seem that in his theory of human nature Shang Yang was right and the author of *The Great Learning*, along with Meng Hsien Tzu, was wrong. This is doubly clear when societies become industrial as well as agricultural communities. The old traditions of tribal honour, the old codes of chivalry to the weak, fall into decay, and the materialistic realist, whether he be a Conservative defending a privilege or a Marxian Socialist denouncing it, can make his case for a mechanical dialectic in man's social history. It always has been so, and perhaps it always will be so.

On the other hand, the extraordinary thing is that Karl Marx found himself driven one stage further to a profoundly illogical conclusion. He prophesied that when the Have-nots have destroyed the Haves, then an equilibrium of peace and prosperity will emerge. This is idealism in the deliberately materialistic mind, and a fatal idealism at that. The problems of human relationships are not solved automatically by any social adjustments achieved by covetous animals. Human-heartedness in the individual and a general will in the community, these are indispensable.

Thus, modern man is on the horns of a dilemma. He cannot trust the old morality of the gentleman, for it breaks down under the pressure of civilized conditions. Neither can he trust the totalitarian efficiency State with its forests of regulations and armies of 'robbing experts.' Thus the term 'Great Learning' takes on a new meaning, namely the great process of learning to which mankind is forced to commit itself.

Confucius's grandson maintained that some men learn by hard experience, others in easier ways. He understated the case; for the vast majority learn through bitter experience. Only the few are so happy—and so unfortunate—as to learn easily. And experience is, in relation to heaven and earth, amongst those things which bring so great profit to man. But there is also experience in relation to Heaven, the supernatural element in Nature, the mysterious Will which emerges relating Man to Nature and Nature to Man. By it a change comes into view, an authoritative direction, a spiritual law by the observance of which man escapes some of the bitter experiences of failure.

Each generation has the opportunity to start nearer the good life for man than the generation before it.

This law of Heaven may be expressed in more ways than one, but to the realistic mind there is something peculiarly satisfying in Confucius's expression of it as reciprocity. For in regard to man's relationship with Nature, he must give to Nature if he is to receive from her, as he must receive from Nature if he is to give to her. So also in his relations with men, giving and receiving go hand in hand. Further, whereas in this reciprocal relationship with Nature there is the fact of compulsion if man is to sustain life at any but the lowest level, in the reciprocal relations between men, compulsion takes him only a very little way. The power of free giving and free receiving has become a great part of man's heritage. And this power is characteristic of the self in flower. For as free giving and free receiving bring the self into flower, so that self is the more able to give and to receive.

Such a process of self-enrichment, which at the same time reaches out to the enrichment of the selves of others, would appear to have no limit, except the limit of death. That surely stops the process, for the sage, like other men, goes hence, and his place knows him no more. To this the authors of these two books make answer: the power of personality does not cease with death. There is a Reality in Heaven, and the sage and the saint prove this reality in man. This Reality, or realness on the way to being reality, cannot be intermittent, nor can it die.

APPENDICES

I

LEIBNIZ AND CHU HSI

THE only passage I know of which contains a definite statement by Leibniz himself as to the sources of his system is the one the reader can find quoted in Latta's *Leibniz*: 'This system appears to combine Plato with Democritus, Aristotle with Descartes, the Scholastics with the moderns, theology and ethics with reason. It seems to take the best from all sides, and then to go further than any one has yet gone . . .':[1] a tantalizing statement with its 'appears' and 'seems,' even though he goes on to define what he means. Adolph Reichwein, in his *China and Europe*, would have us believe that in the doctrine of the Monads we have 'Chinese ideas about "the universal" as they are expressed in the three great exponents of Chinese life, in Lao Tzu, in Confucius, and in the Chinese form of Buddhism.'[2] That is doubtless true in a sense, but a sense so wide that it leaves the historian with a strong feeling of dissatisfaction. It is here maintained that we can go a good deal further in the way of defining the coincidences. Since we know that Leibniz read *Confucius, Sinarum Philosophus*, and since

[1] Op cit., p. 155 (1925 impression). The passage is taken from *Nouveaux Essais sur l'Entendement humain*. It were well to give Leibniz's own words at one point: 'Il semble qu'il prend le meilleur de tous côtés, et que puis après il va plus loin qu'on n'est allé encore.' Also the succeeding sentences which Latta has omitted: 'J'y trouve une explication intelligible de l'union de l'ame et du corps, chose dont j'avois désespéré auparavant. Je trouve les vrais principes des choses dans les unités des Substances, que ce Système introduit, et dans leur harmonie prééstablie par la Substance primitive. J'y trouve une simplicité et une uniformité surprenante, en sort qu'on peut dire que c'est partout et toujours la même chose, aux dégrés de perfection près.'

[2] Unfortunately, he does not explain this in sufficient detail to enable us to appreciate what he had in mind. My own examination leads me to the conclusion that the resemblances are only general and vague in this connection. But perhaps we have much the same material in mind, and the explanation of our disagreement lies in the fact that Chu Hsi's philosophy shows definite signs of Taoist and Buddhist influence.

that work is, generally speaking, Neo-Confucianist in its interpretations, what precisely is the extent of coincidence between Leibniz's monadology and Chu Hsi's *li hsüeh*? The following is an outline of what he meant by *li*; and, in order that the reader may the more easily substitute a monad as he reads, I have added Leibniz's non-coinciding ideas in brackets and put Chu Hsi's non-coinciding ones in italics.

Li is that unitary (unanalysable because) indivisible something inherent in everything and every man, *and in every species of thing* as it is in mankind, the highest species of animal-thing. This makes everything what it is both in itself and in relation to all other things. *Li* was in the *T'ai Chi*, Great Beginning (the Great Cause, God), when the universe began, and without *li* there would have been no Great Beginning, for without *li* no thing could exist and there would be no universe at all. *Li* is outside of time and space, and therefore was in existence before the universe, *but this is not the case with the Yin-yang and the Five Hsing which are the dynamic and* (?) *chemical media through which ch'i* (*matter*) *achieves form in every distinctive thing*. *Li* is not in the form but is the order of the compound which a thing is. *Li* is not subject to the ceaseless changes in time and space which are characteristic of things and which come from the existence of matter in them. Since *li* itself does not change, it abides through all changes, but in speaking of it as abiding, care must be taken to avoid thinking of it as resting in contrast to moving, because rest and movement are strictly relative to each other in space (as is to be seen in the Infinite Calculus, which shows rest as the minimum of movement). So also in time is-ness and becoming-ness are relative to each other. Man's *li* is to be seen in his nature, just as the *li* of everything is in its nature; and the essence of man's nature is a capacity for humanity, justice, mutual deference, and knowledge (love and wisdom). This goodness has existed from the Great Beginning, but *ch'i* through the passions acts in man so as to obscure goodness, and it is sages who have ordered this force of *ch'i* in man so that man comes to shine forth in his perfection, that perfection which is the complete actualization of *li*. Thus through *li* there are *ho* (convenience) and unity in the universe.

Apart from Leibniz's emphasis on the existence of a Living God there would seem to be little that a disciple of his would wish to change or add. The *Yin-yang* and the Five *Hsing* need not worry us, since the former was the classical Confucianist expression for the element of relativity in physical existence, a phenomenon of which Leibniz was fully conscious. The latter was a crude attempt at scientific analysis of the universe, making thereby Five Physical Forces (water, fire, metal, wood, and earth): a section of Chu Hsi's thought which does not fit particularly well into his main system.

On the other hand, its presence there opens up a very large question. Thus, I said Five Physical Forces, not four elements, such as we find in early Greek speculation. The interesting thing is that, whereas the Five *Hsing* (lit. activities) were essentially dynamic in Chinese classical thought, in Chu Hsi they show signs of being chemical, that is to say, chemical elements in things rather than physical forces. He makes room for *chih* (raw material) alongside of *ch'i*, which is the more refined part of the stuff of the universe. His mind appears to be struggling to get the idea of 'substance,' and in this way he gets near to it. The student, however, must beware of assuming that because Chu Hsi's *li* corresponds in so many particulars with Leibniz's monad, therefore Leibniz's definition of a monad as a simple substance in the thing, the compound substance, is one which Chu Hsi would have understood. He might, but I think it is doubtful. The point here is the one on which a contemporary Chinese philosopher has recently made a statement. It is that in the West, owing to its belief in a Personal God, metaphysics always finds reality in substance, but that in China, owing to its lack of belief in a Personal God, reality is in relation. I am inclined to think that Professor Chang pushes this too far, but there is undoubtedly a great deal of truth in it. If Chu Hsi doubtfully opened a door to a metaphysic of substance, Leibniz may be taken with much more confidence to have opened the door to a metaphysic of relation as well as of substance.

In conclusion, Latta and Bertrand Russell[1] have both passed severe strictures on Leibniz for the weak logic in his arguments for the existence of God. Mr. Russell is quite sure, I gather, that with the mind Leibniz had he ought to have been a necessitarian; and I presume he would feel the same about Chu Hsi. Part of Mr. Russell's interest and importance for us here is that having analysed Leibniz's arguments on God into four kinds, the Ontological Argument, the Cosmological Argument, the Argument from Eternal Truths, and the Argument from Pre-established Harmony, he goes on to say: 'Only one of these was invented by him (viz. the last), and that was the worst of the four.' In Section 114 he explains that this argument 'is a particular form of the so-called physico-theological proof, otherwise known as the argument from design.' I admit that it sometimes looks like that, but I should have thought that the basic feature of Leibniz's system was not an inference as to design but an *a priori* assumption as to the reality of individuality in things and personality in men, this reality being a spiritual phenomenon. Having assumed that, it seems to me that Leibniz very reasonably assumed that all his things and men in the universe with their monad centres of individuality did not live in a state of real internecine warfare. He made the inference accordingly that there was a pre-established harmony, and since harmony involves the idea of somebody free to harmonize to the utmost, he came to the idea of the Great Harmonizer. And, since the harmony which is in existence is complete only along certain lines and very imperfect along certain other lines, he made the inference that in addition to the sphere of necessity there was a sphere of contingency. This basic assumption of reality in personality existing in

[1] *The Philosophy of Leibniz.* London, second edition, 1937.

a universe of the necessary and the contingent is a distinctive feature of Confucianist philosophy from the time when Confucius taught and his followers made *The Mean-in-action* and *The Great Learning*.

II

LIST OF SUSPICIOUSLY LATE TERMS IN THE SUSPECT SECTIONS OF 'THE MEAN-IN-ACTION'

(The Chu Hsi chapter numbers are used.)

(c. 1.) *Hsing* in its two contexts strikes me as involving the later Mencian view of man's nature as good.

Hsiu tao chih wei chiao: both *hsiu tao* and *chiao* are late highbrow expressions.

Chun tzu shen ch'i tu yeh: this seems to me to come here with just the stock force that it has in third century B.C. books. I doubt whether it became a current phrase before the new age was several generations old.

Chung tse: a double-barrelled expression for a virtue.

T'ien hsia chih ta tao yeh: I doubt if *ta* was used with *tao* and had *t'ien hsia* added on until all the different schools of thought had got going in the fourth century B.C.

(c. 26, second half.) *Shih chao chao chih to;* cp. *yi shao chih to:* this use of *to* as an abstract noun. Cp. also *Wen Wang chih te chih chun*.

Hua yao: this looks like a reference to the sacred Hua Mountain in Shensi; cp. Feng Yu-lan in Bodde's translation, p. 370. The suspicion here is not in relation to date but to which part of the country the writer lived in. Professor Feng's argument is that a Lu State man would hardly ignore his own sacred Tai Mountain and refer to the distant Hua Mountain. The list of scaly inhabitants of the deep is suspiciously late. The reference would appear to be to the more southerly waters of the China Sea.

Kai yueh: a logician's term; cp. *Hsun Tzu*, e.g. *Li Lun* chapter, and the *Wen Yen* of the *Yi Scripture*. The *Wen Yen* is more and more coming to be regarded as a third-century amplification of the original *Yi*.

(c. 27.) *Li yi san pai, wei yi san ch'ien:* cp. *Li Ch'i*, II, 1, in the *Li Chi* and the summary on Li works in the *Yi Wen Chih* of the *Ch'ien Han Shu*. It is not impossible, of course, that such an expression should have been early in use in Ju circles, but since we have only two such late examples, it is, at least, under suspicion here. *Wei yi* comes in the *Tso Chuan*.

Ch'i jen: cp. *Hsun Tzu*, Chapter I.

Chin cheng wei: the three together have a late air.

(c. 28.) This contains the references to the weights and measures, etc.

(c. 29.) The omission of *tse* between two clauses of a series in which the movement of thought is 'if A, then B; if B, then C.' Cp. Introduction, Chapter IV.

K'ao chu san wang erh pu ming, together with the succeeding three parallel clauses, has a quite sophisticated ring; and the last clause, with its reference to waiting a hundred generations for a sage to appear, is specially suspicious.

Tsao yu yü: cp. note *ad hoc* in the translation.

(c. 30.) This shows an advanced stage in the idealization of Confucius, with several suspicious phrases.

(c. 31.) Contains the list of double-barrelled virtues; cp. Introduction, Chapter IV. Some of the words used in the list are very suspicious, e.g. *jui chih* and *wen li*. Further, later in the chapter come *Chung Kuo* for 'China,' and *fan yu hsüeh ch'i chieh* for 'all men.'

(c. 33.) *An jan . . . ti jan.*

Tan erh yen . . . wen erh li: with the succeeding sentence showing Taoist influence and so unlikely in a Confucianist's mouth before the third century B.C.

III

TZU SSU IN 'MENCIUS' AND THE 'T'AN KUNG' OF THE 'LI CHI'

There are six references to Tzu Ssu in *Mencius*, and one passage of eighty-four characters in length which is practically a doublet of a passage to c. 20 (Chu Hsi's chapter number) of *The Mean-in-action*. There are also six anecdotes about Tzu Ssu in the *T'an Kung*. Hsun Ch'ing in his book (*Hsun Tzu*) refers to Tzu Ssu and Mencius together as notable disciples of Confucius, but as not understanding his teaching aright. It would appear that Hsun Ch'ing regarded Mencius as belonging to a Tzu Ssu section in the Confucianist school. For this reason the evidence in *Mencius* is of first-rate importance.

This evidence is both illuminating and puzzling. On the one hand, the doublet passage (*Mencius*, IV, a, 12) has the key word *ch'eng* in it and makes the same distinction between the actual, entire *ch'eng*-ness of Heaven and the embryo, on-the-way *ch'eng*-ness of man. In other respects also Mencius's mind is in affinity with Tzu Ssu's, e.g. in a recognition of the relativity of the material universe and the clear distinction to be made between Heaven, the benevolent Will towards man, and the material heaven and earth. On the other hand, Mencius does not acknowledge Tzu Ssu (or anybody else) as the author of this passage. Nor in his anecdotes about Tzu Ssu is there any sign of his being regarded by Mencius as his teacher or anything more than a Ju of repute. Also, the doublet is puzzling, because in some respects the wording is slightly different, and because *ch'eng* in the philosophic sense does not occur again in Mencius's book. It is used in the purely popular sense which we find in the *Book of Songs* and the *Analects*: as we should say of an event, 'truly' or 'really' it was so.

There is a real doubt, therefore, whether Mencius would have acknowledged himself as a disciple of Tzu Ssu. We have, however, in this matter to appreciate the fact that Mencius had an extremely independent nature, which he showed in various ways, one of them being his independent way of quoting Confucius to suit his own theories. Taking everything into account, we need not reject Hsun Ch'ing's evidence of a connection between the two men. It is perhaps characteristic of their relation that Tzu Ssu emphasized in true philosophic vein that the Way of the Mean is as much the Way for the common man as for the sage, whilst Mencius made a political application of this doctrine.

Mencius, indeed, was a political theorist and a psychologist, whilst Tzu Ssu was a philosopher, and a metaphysician at that.

The other early references to Tzu Ssu, namely those in the *T'an Kung*, all harmonize with each other. They emphasize a professional, ritual-expertise side to him. They are, therefore, not particularly helpful except in two respects. One is that Tzu Ssu is shown as intimate with Tseng Ts'an, the arch filial pietist. That is in harmony with the emphasis on filial piety in the A part of *The Mean-in-action*. We may imagine our philosopher coming to the conclusion that the common man had better stick to filial piety at all costs. The other respect is that one passage represents Tzu Ssu as using the term *ch'eng*, though not in the philosophic sense of reality.

IV

'WU-WEI' (TAKES NO ACTION) IN 'THE MEAN-IN-ACTION,' SECTION XI

It is impossible here to go into the intricacies of the controversy which has arisen in relation to the earliest literary expressions of Taoist beliefs. I can only state my own position. It is that I agree with those critics who regard the *Tao Te Ching* (cp. Waley, *The Way and its Power*) not as the work of Lao Tzu, the contemporary of Confucius, but as a composite work containing earlier and later materials. It was probably not put together before the third century B.C. (Cp. Feng Yu-lan in Bodde's translation, *A History of Chinese Philosophy*, Chapter XIII.) That being so, the authentic chapters in *Chuang Tzu* are the earliest Taoist writings we can date with even rough accuracy. If, however, those chapters be taken as the earliest expressions of Taoist opinions, they create a difficulty. They show such extraordinary maturity of expression and conviction that it is difficult to believe that Chuang Chou (369–?286 B.C.) was the first of the great Taoists. He unquestionably had a brilliant intellect; but even so!

We read of hermits in the fifth century B.C.; cp. *Analects, passim.* And passages in the *Tao Te Ching* look as if they had a history behind them. Also, hermits may have profound thoughts but no means of popularizing them, so we need not wonder if the first Taoists did not get into print, so to speak. None the less, there is the question how Chuang Chou's mind was stimulated by other influences, e.g. earlier books. I make the suggestion, therefore, that perhaps Tzu Ssu was the first man to think of *wu-wei*, the expression for the waiting activity of the soul, the inactivity which is more real than any purposeful activity can be. I can discover no reason why he should not have thought of this, and certainly the expression of such a sentiment in this passage is not incompatible with the rest of his tenets.

V

'CHUNG KUO,' THE MIDDLE KINGDOM: 'THE MEAN-IN-ACTION', SECTION XVII, AND 'THE GREAT LEARNING,' SECTION VII, 4.

It is a very arguable case that this expression for China did not exist before there was a united China, i.e. at earliest in the time of the First Emperor's reign. The common expression for the whole society of Chou states in North China was, as has been stated, *t'ien hsia* (heaven below), which I have been translating as 'the Great Society.' I suggest that when the new age of reasoning had got fully under way, namely by the fourth century B.C., the consciousness in the new kind of scholar-administrator of their society as possessing a superior civilization became considerably accentuated. This, plus the range of ideas about the Way of the Mean (*Chung*), would create a situation in which the Middle Kingdom would be a natural expression of cultural unity. *Kuo* admittedly came to mean a state as distinct from a *pang* (region), but none of the states in the late Chou centuries had a very permanent border, so that *kuo* may have been used to denote a large cultural area, unified in that sense. In view of Chu State being only semi-Chinese culturally speaking, and politically not part of the original Chou order, it would appear possible that the term *Chung Kuo* might have been coined about the time of Chu's expansion and used by politicians who wished to convey the meaning that Chu was, after all, only a barbarian country. I am not satisfied, therefore, that the term was not in use before the First Emperor's time.

VI

ROUSSEAU AND NATURE IN FAMILY RELATIONS

The sentiments in Section VI (p. 157) remind us vividly of Rousseau in his hermit stage, when he was writing letters to the young ladies of his acquaintance preparing them for married life; cp. also the *Nouvelle Héloïse*. I suppose a case could be made out proving more or less adequately that his experience with Madame de Warens and then with Thérèse le Vasseur produced the passion he had for Nature in family relationships. But M. Maritain's strictures on Rousseau, prejudiced though they are, yet have this amount of truth in them that they make us pause in this matter. Personally I am not satisfied that Rousseau's experiences with women do at all necessarily, or even naturally, explain the extremely new ideas he came to put forth about Nature in relation to family life. The explanation usually given involves some highly dubious assumptions in the fields of religious and sex psychology. Surely it was in the life of his mind, in the ideas which laid hold of him, that he found refuge from his devastating sensibilities. On that ground I suggest that it is significant that in Du Halde's famous work which was published in Paris in 1735, and which we know was read by, at any rate, one of the Encyclopaedists, Voltaire, there should be a summary of *The Great Learning*, and in that summary the following words: 'Love your People as a tender Mother loves her Child, which affection is inspired by Nature and requires no study; for it was never known that a Maid, before she was married, studied how she ought to behave herself when she gave her Child suck.' (English translation, 1736, vol. iii, p. 305.)